Laundry Tales

"To Lighten Your Load"™

Melissa Howell, Angie Peters

& the Celebrate Moms Team

Evergreen PRESS

Mobile, Alabama

Laundry Tales To Lighten Your Load
Melissa Howell and Angie Peters, general editors
Copyright © 2007 Celebrate Moms, Inc.

ISBN 978-1-58169-245-7
For Worldwide Distribution
Printed in the U.S.A.

Evergreen Press
P.O. Box 191540 • Mobile, AL 36619

Table of Contents

Dedication

To our fellow laundry-toting, carpooling,
nose-wiping, baby-burping moms—
and the families they so proudly
and humbly serve.

Acknowledgments

Now, our God, we give you thanks, and praise your glorious name (1 Chronicles 29:13).

A special thanks is in order for all who helped bring this book to fruition:

• Dena Dyer—we'll never forget our brainstorming session that sparked the idea for *Laundry Tales*.

• The Celebrate Moms' Team and their families, especially our husbands, who so humbly—and without complaint—pulled double parenting shifts as we were tucked away in our offices.

• The staff of CLASServices—your training and support through the years have been invaluable.

• All the great people at Evergreen Press—thank you for believing in us!

• Our special guest contributors and their families.

• The online community of Celebrate Moms—you are the inspiration for everything we do.

Thank you!

Introduction

When I opened the dryer door, a kaleidoscope of every shade of blue imaginable enveloped my eyes. The only problem was, this was a load of whites! My mind reverted back to an earlier phone call between my husband and our three year old daughter, Cammie.

"Daddy, me made sumptin for eww!" She could barely contain the excitement as she continued, "It's bwue and me cowored it awe by myself."

Evidently, the color of the day in her pre-school class was blue. She was so proud of her creation, she pocketed the crayon in hopes of coloring more pictures at home. If only I had checked her pockets before laundering her clothes. . . .

Does this scenario sound familiar? As I shared this story with my friends and the Celebrate Moms online community, they began telling me stories of their own laundry disasters.

It's a fact: Mothers everywhere are struggling to keep up with the laundry and often find it impossible to delight in such a mundane chore. *Laundry Tales to Lighten Your Load* uses real-life stories to share the comical, somber, and sometimes poignant episodes experienced in the laundry room and the valuable truths learned through them.

It is our prayer that, through this book, you will gain a sense of camaraderie with other mothers everywhere and realize—as isolated as you may feel at times—you are not alone. We are all right beside you—soaking, pre-treating, washing, drying, folding, and putting away our own freshly cleaned laundry.

Happy Laundering!

—*Melissa Howell*

SECTION 1

Lost, Shrunk, or Stolen?

WASHTIME WOES

Jami Kirkbride

"Now what?" my husband asked as he looked at me lying on the couch, oblivious to all around me.

"Put 'em in the washer," I mumbled. The morning sickness kept me from wanting to open my mouth for fear of what might happen.

"Wait, did you separate them?" I asked, a little panicked at the thought of his doing the laundry for the first time. He looked around the corner at me with his arms full of dirty clothes ready to shove into the washer.

"Yeah," he nodded, as though that was a silly question. "These are dirty, and the others are not!"

I knew then that we were in trouble. My wonderful husband does many things well. In fact, he is probably the smartest person I know. But, bless his heart, he had no clue about how to do laundry. (His mother had taken such good care of him that, as I remember, she had even done a load of laundry for him the day before we married.)

Now I was pregnant with our second child. Loads of laundry had spread into nearly every room, and I could barely move off the couch. My body was not adjusting well to the hormonal changes and appeared to be staging a revolt. I did as much as I could, but it was a far cry from the usual.

"Don't worry," my husband offered graciously. "I can help."

I explained the sorting process in brief, then drifted off to sleep. I awoke to discover a slightly altered maternity wardrobe. My jeans had been washed in hot water and machine dried, not hung—spelling trouble for a long-legged person like me. My nice new winter capris would now squeeze uncomfortably around my middle, barely stretching across the massive mound of baby I was carrying. And my toothpick-thin long legs would protrude conspicuously from the bottom of my newly shortened slacks. Even my shirt, which had once resembled a tent, now had three-quarter length sleeves instead of full length. I may have been able to pull off wearing it if the shirt had remained long enough to cover my tummy, which would now be exposed above the top of my shrunken pants.

I swallowed hard and bit my lip. I didn't want to say a word. My husband had tried so hard, and I didn't want him to think I hadn't appreciated his help. "Hey!" he popped his head around the doorway, "I got three loads done!"

"I see," I said, as thoughts of other ruined outfits flitted through my mind. "Thanks."

At that very moment, I decided to count my blessings—a strategy that has proven helpful throughout the course of our marriage. Focusing on being thankful that my husband is willing to help doesn't ensure everything will be done the way I would do it. But it does change my perspective. I no longer see what he does as being wrong . . . just different.

LOAD LIGHTENER
April 15th is Husband Appreciation Day. Have you taken time to thank your husband for the things he does to help? This would be a great opportunity for you to voice your appreciation, even for the things he doesn't do quite like you!

Jami Kirkbride lives on a Wyoming ranch. Her inspiration comes from everyday adventures with her husband Jeff and their four children.

3

DIDN'T BRING IT? DON'T NEED IT!

Anna Marie Warren

Aahh, the sound of the water rushing in and out and the feeling of the warm breeze as it moves around my face. Perhaps you have heard and felt it, too—the unmistakable sensation of being lost in the sea of laundry that has to be done before the family leaves on vacation.

Where does it all come from? Loads and loads of washing, drying, and ironing must be done before departure. So many clothes, so little time.

My husband, an efficient packer who always makes a list and never forgets a thing, is always getting on to my four daughters and me because we take far too many clothes on our vacations—especially for trips to the beach.

"All you need is a bathing suit, shorts, and flip-flops," he tells us. To prove his point, on a recent trip he limited each of us to one bag per person.

We just couldn't fathom accomplishing this impossible feat. What kind of vacation was this going to be without a different outfit for each mood, a different pair of flip-flops for each outfit, and a different cover-up for each swimsuit? After much sulking, we stepped up to the challenge, figuring we probably wouldn't see anyone who knew us anyway. We determined to forget about fashion statements and focus on fun in the sun. (We also secretly agreed to go "souvenir shopping" for clothes while we were at the beach. After all, my husband said we could only take one bag with us—but he didn't say how many bags we could bring back home!)

The six-hour drive to the beach gave us girls ample time in which to complain about the things we couldn't bring along because of our one-bag limit. A man of few words, my husband only responded with one statement: "If you didn't bring it, you don't need it!"

4

Once at the beach, we jumped out of the station wagon and began hauling our bags up the stairs into the cabin. Soon the car was unloaded, and we began to unwind and plan our week of adventure. Of course, we girls couldn't help but discuss what we would wear for each activity. Again, my husband reminded us: "If you didn't bring it, you don't need it!"

As nighttime approached, after the girls and I finished our last game of Scrabble, we stepped onto the cabin deck to take in the view of the moonlit ocean, thinking, *nothing could be better than this.* Nothing, that is, except the moan from my husband inside the cabin as he declared that he had forgotten something.

This was big news, considering it came from the man who never forgets a thing! When we ran inside for the details, he reluctantly told us what he had left behind: his underwear.

Not surprisingly, the only words of comfort we could think to offer were familiar: "If you didn't bring it, you don't need it!"

LOAD LIGHTENER

The best way to prepare for a family outing is to have every family member write out a detailed list of everything needed for the trip, then use that as a packing checklist. This will eliminate the chance of overlooking the essentials.

Anna Marie Warren is a Celebrate Moms' Team Member and lives in Texas.

5

INNOCENCE LOST, CHARACTER FORMED

Sandy McKeown

If Eve hadn't taken that first bite, would we be doing laundry? I don't think the pain of childbirth was the only judgment declared on women that fateful day. How long did it take Eve to realize the Designer clothes, which she and Adam had been given to cover their newly realized nakedness, needed proper care? Did she plan ahead and fashion another animal skin skirt instead of washing the one she was wearing? Or did she go down to the stream and gently dip into the clear running water to cool off one day and watch astonished as the water shrunk her hand-clean-with-other-skins-only outfit? She didn't have that problem before the snake talked her into a taste of the apple.

By definition, launder means to wash and iron clothes, but it also has a secondary connotation—to disguise the true nature of an act. My Bible commentary also describes the snake as an unclean creature. So it all points back to laundry. No wonder women hate snakes—it's because of them we do laundry.

The task of gathering dirty clothing scattered throughout the house and carrying them to an often dingy work area to sort, pre-soak, wash, dry, fold, mend, iron, and return to their proper locations—and then do it all again in a few days—is the essence of drudgery. Menial hard work is something most all of us would like to avoid, but notice what biblical scholar Oswald Chambers writes on the subject: "Drudgery is one of the finest touchstones of character there is."

If drudgery truly refines one's character, women must have loads of character. Performing the simple task of doing laundry for our families day in and day out defines us as more than ordinary. We are women who, in those moments, are compliantly carrying out a needed task that serves our family. Just as Jesus knelt at the feet of his disciples to humbly wash the dirt off their well-traveled soles in servitude, we submissively stand at the rubber-footed feet of our washers and dryers to clean the dirt off the clothes for the souls we serve. We do so partly to get our offspring properly clothed again. But an even more worthy result of this chore is seizing the opportunity to be role models of serving others for our growing children to follow.

When one of my children walks into the laundry room and innocently asks, "Whatcha doin'?" I can respond with a hasty retort that would be natural for a self-imposed martyr: "Laundry. What does it look like I'm doing?" Or, I can boast I am refining my character through the daily drudgery of serving our family's needs via menial work. Or, I can reach even higher and respond, "I'm being blessed by loving you."

My neighbor's newer washing machine was not draining water recently, which required a call to the local repairman. He discovered a snake wedged in the drain hose, plugging the machine's ability to drain the water properly. My neighbors speculated the wife picked up her husband's gardening gloves from the grass in the back yard and threw them into the washing machine—undetected and unclean creature and all. If it had been me who had picked up those gloves, I would have thrown them down the laundry chute—and washed them a week later with the rest of the clothes at the bottom of the chute. I'd either have found a mad snake or a dead snake, neither of which sounds appealing. Snakes and laundry shouldn't mix!

I wonder if, after Eve realized she had to trudge down to the stream every Monday morning to get those animal prints clean, any snake that dared slither past would be seized by its scaly tail and angrily swung against her laundry rock.

Focusing merely on getting the laundry clean disguises the true nature of the task. The snake did talk Eve into taking that first bite, taking away the innocence of mankind; but despite that deceptive act, the opportunity remains to love others through our actions, just as Jesus did. It's character refinement at its best.

LAUNDRY'S LIFE LESSON
"Drudgery is one of the finest touchstones of character there is." —Oswald Chambers

Sandy McKeown is a Celebrate Moms' Team Member and lives in Iowa.

MISSING DIRTY SOCKS

Connie Pombo

"Mom, have you seen my tennis socks?" Jon's cry for help was a familiar one. Lost socks—clean or dirty—have been a part of my laundry landscape for as long as I can remember. But these socks were special. They were supposed to be taking a big trip. We had loaded up the car that morning and were heading west—Grove City, Pennsylvania, that is—the place where my youngest son would be spending the next four years at college. His sheets, towels, notebooks, and tennis racquet were all crossed off the list. The only missing item: a pair of socks.

"Did you check in the washer and dryer?"

"Yes, I checked there first." My son's voice sounded a little irritated that I would even suggest the most obvious of all places. But that's exactly where many "lost and found" items had turned up in the past 18 years.

I wandered back into Jon's room to scout for the missing pair. The room was bare except for a wadded-up pair of dirty tennis socks in the corner near his closet. How could something so obvious be missed?

As I surveyed the empty room, I thought of all the socks I had laundered and folded over the years: the blue booties that I carefully washed by hand, the Little League socks with ground-in dirt, the grass-stained soccer socks that almost made it to the state championship, and now Jon's tennis socks caked with remnants of clay dirt. All those dirty socks represented a lifetime of love and nurturing, and now they were going to be missed. Tears fell freely as I plopped myself down on his bed. It was the end of one phase—meaning one less laundry basket—and the beginning of a new life, the empty nest.

My pity party was cut short when Jon bounded down the stairs into the bedroom. "Come on, Mom, we're going to be late!"

I held the dirty—now muddy—socks in my hands and dabbed my tears.

"Oh, Mom, please don't cry . . . it's going to be okay. I'll be back for Thanksgiving." Jon—not given to great displays of affection—wrapped his arms around me and patted me on the back. I held on tightly and then let go. "Here's your socks, Jon, and remember to keep the whites and darks separate when you wash them—okay?"

He grinned and said, "I know, Mom, I watched you."

We as parents often don't consider ourselves as mentors, but we are the greatest mentors our children will ever know. We spend time with them, train them, and watch the seeds of God's love grow in their hearts. I have been my kids' coach, best friend, and teacher—that's what a mentor is. Hopefully, the seeds planted in their childhood will continue to grow—dirty socks and all!

SUDSY SUGGESTION

Here is my recipe for white socks: Pour about 1-1/2 gallons of water into a 2-gallon pot; heat to boiling. Remove from heat; add three scoops of OxyClean and place the socks (wet them first) into the solution to soak for up to six hours, stirring occasionally with a stainless-steel, slotted spoon. Drain the socks into a colander; wash as usual. The result: brilliantly clean, white socks!

Connie Pombo is an author, speaker, and founder of Women's Mentoring Ministries in Mt. Joy, Pennsylvania. Her greatest accomplishment, however, is being mom to her two grown sons.

DRY CLEAN ONLY

Marilyn Nutter

Katie struggled to stretch her sweater, but it hardly reached her waist. I concluded that the sweater would probably fit a chimpanzee, with the front and back extremely short and the arms disproportionately long. My daughter held the misshapen garment up with a puzzled look.

"I washed it in cold water," she said. "Just like the other one. What happened?"

"Did you read the label?" I asked.

"No, I figured that all of my sweaters could be washed on the cold setting."

"I know that it won't help this time, but let's check the label," I said, trying to console her. "This one says 'dry clean only.' Sometimes sweaters are 'hand wash only in cold or warm water,' and sometimes they say 'dry clean only.' Now next time, you'll remember to read labels and instructions first so that you won't automatically put clothes into the washing machine."

Disappointed, she tossed the sweater into the trash. At dinner we discussed Katie's "tragic event," as she put it.

"That's too bad," my husband said. "It sounds just like the time my sweater vests came out of the wash. They could have fit a six-year-old."

Katie knew her dad did his own laundry when he was a college student, but she had never heard this story.

"Oh you did the same thing when you were living in the dorms?" Katie asked, fascinated by the revelation.

My husband paused, and the expression on his face developed into a smile. "Not exactly," he answered.

"Well, how did it happen?" By this time, Katie was pressing for information, and my husband complied.

"It was your mother who washed my sweater vests," he said. "They were 'dry clean only' too." He looked at me, and we laughed.

He was right. I had assumed the vests were washable, but they weren't. Recalling the incident made me think about the teachable "dry clean only" moments in our lives. The labels on the sweaters had instructions and information designed to give appropriate results. Katie's limited knowledge gave me an opportunity for a lesson on laundry and dry cleaning. She now knows to read labels before throwing anything into the washing machine. (She also knows that her mother makes mistakes too!)

Moms have many teachable moments. These opportunities may pop up during a walk with one of our kids, while we're watching TV, when we're dealing with the fall-out of a mistake, when we're discussing lessons learned from relationships, and when we're affirming good choices.

We moms have our own personal teachable moments too, as we respond to what we read in the Bible, as we experience the consequences of both our poor and wise choices, and as we learn lessons about ourselves.

Katie and I learned from our laundry catastrophes so that we wouldn't repeat our mistakes. I taught Katie about the importance of reading labels before she does laundry, but reading and responding to teachable moments and life-changing labels? Well, that's what it's really all about.

LOAD LIGHTENER

A teachable moment is a situation that opens a door for a conversation with your child. Listening to song lyrics, passing a billboard, watching a TV commercial, and discussing decisions are just a few opportunities to help you understand your child's thoughts and opinions.

Lost, Shrunk, or Stolen?

LAUNDRY'S LIFE LESSON

The invention of dry cleaning occurred by accident when a French tailor unintentionally knocked over a paraffin lamp, spilling its contents onto a stained tablecloth. After drying, the stains disappeared and stain removal through "dry cleaning" was born.

Marilyn Nutter and her husband of thirty-seven years live in western Pennsylvania. Marilyn is the author of Dressed up Moms' Devotions to Go (2006) *and* Tea Lovers' Devotions to Go (2007).

SECTION 2

Unusual Discoveries

PICKING POCKETS

Marilyn Rockett

Oh no, not again! As I pulled a pair of jeans from the dryer, I gasped at the red blotches across the faded denim of my son's pants—evidence of an undiscovered crayon buried in a pocket. Now I faced a salvage job if those jeans were to be wearable another day.

We washed lots of jeans in our household of four boys. Interesting little tidbits tucked deep in the pockets were inevitable discoveries. Those small treasures represented some passion or momentary interest of the wearer. Each prize was special, deserving an important place in its owner's pocket as he explored the world around him, learning and inventing. These unique assets and life collections helped define my sons' boyhoods. They discovered, dreamed, and dared as they added to their precious assortment.

I wanted my sons to grow and explore. However, those collections also presented practical concerns—loss of good clothing from irreparable messes, precious time spent remedying the errors, and training my sons to take responsibility for their possessions. I needed a solution, and my constant nagging reminders were not working . . . as if they ever do!

How's a mother to train noisy, messy, adventurous boys? It was a challenge that called for a firm but fair method. I began by reminding the boys (only once before each laundry day) to empty their pockets before tossing the jeans into the laundry hamper, allowing them the opportunity to redeem themselves if they forgot. Then I parked two containers conspicuously on a shelf above my washing machine.

On washday, I carefully checked each pocket. Coins I

16

found went into one of the containers—my pay for doing their pocket-emptying job. Into another container went any toy or object that was valuable, monetarily or otherwise: small cars, a stray Lego, a special collectible. To redeem the lost treasure, the forgetful boy had to do an extra chore. I usually did not use giving chores for punishment lest they learn to hate work, but I was training forgetful boys, not punishing malicious ones. This was a lesson in accepting consequences for a decision or action and working for what they wanted. Any object I deemed trash (and there were numerous items in that category) went into the wastebasket; it was the owner's loss.

Why is training children to empty their pockets important? Why not just let boyish forgetfulness slide? It's in the little things—in our children's lives and in our own—that we learn the big lessons of life. We learn respect for our possessions and for other people. We learn that others aren't always available to clean up our messes, and we learn that we should take responsibility for those messes.

Mark Twain once said, "A habit cannot be tossed out the window; it must be coaxed down the stairs a step at a time."[1] Training our kids to take responsibility for little things helps them understand their responsibilities in the larger matters. Scripture teaches us that lesson: "Whoever is faithful in very little is also faithful in much."[2]

Parental consistency, plus my boys' desire to retain their precious possessions, solved the problem in a short while, and I rejoiced over their successfully assuming responsibility. In our home, training my sons to "pick pockets" resulted in well-learned life-lessons.

SUDSY SUGGESTIONS

Did you know that WD-40 gets crayon out of fabric? Go to www.Crayola.com and click on "For Parents/Stain Tips" to find out more ways to remove stains made by such products as crayons, glue, modeling compound, and chalk from clothing, carpeting, upholstery, and other surfaces.

Train your children to help with laundry. Assign different colored plastic laundry baskets to each child or write each child's name on his or her own basket. On laundry day, require your child to bring his or her dirty clothes to the laundry room in that basket. When you and your children fold clothes, place each child's clothes back into his or her basket for putting away. It is easy to tell who neglected laundry duty by seeing which baskets are still full of folded clothes.

Marilyn Rockett—mom, grandmother, author, and speaker—provides organizational help and encouragement in her latest book, Homeschooling at the Speed of Life.

A PRICKLY TALE

Judy Dippel

Having a young child explain something exciting he [or she] has seen is the finest example of communication you will ever hear or see. —Bob Talbert

The laundry room wasn't dull one adventurous day when I was five years old. And for my mom, the surprising hub of events caused her to re-think how carefully she listened to me.

My brother and my dad were gone, and my mom was busy sewing. I wanted to play with the hula-hoop that hung in the laundry room. Opening the door, I took the first step inside, but paused when I heard an odd, scratching sound. Taking the second step into the laundry room, I listened more carefully. Again I heard a strange scraping noise.

The washer and dryer sat silent. What had I heard? Something was in there! The pantry door in the laundry room inched open ever so slightly. Startled, I hurled the hula-hoop aside and ran back into the house to find Mom.

"Come with me, Mom! There's a noise in the laundry room pantry! Something's moving the door. It's a ghost or monster . . . or something!"

Mom continued sewing as she answered calmly, "I'll check it later. Go find something else to do."

I walked back toward the laundry room, curious and determined to find the source of the racket, although I was afraid of what it might be. Listening with my imagination soaring, I heard only silence, but noticed the outside door was ajar. Then I froze. I heard whatever it was moving in the pantry.

What was it?

Within seconds, I raced back up the couple of stairs into the kitchen. Slamming the door behind me, I yelled, "Mom, Mom! There's still something in the laundry room!"

Mom was on the phone. She flashed me the look that said in no uncertain terms, "Later . . . be quiet!"

I went back into the laundry room. Again, silence greeted me, but I noticed dark brown blobs across the top of the white dryer. *Do monsters make droppings?* I wondered. I glanced at the corner. From under the pantry door, a fat, odd-looking tail protruded. It didn't look like any tail I'd ever seen before. Without notice, it disappeared back under the door. Curious, I mustered up my courage and walked over to open the door. When I did, I saw two beady eyes staring right back at me.

The creature was a couple of feet in length, with slender quills covering its back and sides, and fatter quills shielding its tail. I bolted to find Mom again.

"Mom! Mom! The thing is in the pantry. It stared at me, and I slammed the pantry door on it!" Breathless, I spat out the words. "It's this long and this high," I gasped for air, stretching my arms both ways to show her the creature's dimensions. "It's got black eyes, and it's all brown . . . prickly everywhere . . . sharp things—like a monster pincushion. It just stared at me and didn't go away!"

My mother had a quizzical, frightened look on her face. Until recently, she had always been a city girl, and the alarm in her voice was evident. "Do you know what it is?"

Panic-stricken, she called my dad, who came right home. Armed with a baseball bat, he carefully opened the pantry door in the laundry room, where the large "monster" porcupine stood in all its glory, quite unaffected by all our hysteria. Dad reached down with the bat and nudged the slow, clumsy creature out the door, then prodded it on to the edge of the woods, where it scampered off—never to be seen again.

For the porcupine, life went on, but that bat was never quite the same: The thick, bristly quills that lodged in the grain of the bat's wood had left their mark.

I haven't seen a live porcupine since, but the 20 pound rodent visiting our laundry room taught my mom and me both something valuable. I learned about porcupines, and my mom learned that the nonstop talking of her young daughter was sometimes worth listening to.

LAUNDRY'S LIFE LESSONS

Sometimes we put off our kids' demands for attention—especially when we're in the middle of doing something—but we might want to consider stopping, looking, and listening!

Listening to our children takes time, but it's best to do so because the results might be dangerously "prickly" if we don't.

Judy Dippel is a Celebrate Moms' Team Member and lives in Oregon.

WHEN MONEY LAUNDERING IS OK

Heidi J. Krumenauer

Remember when the U.S. Treasury developed the new state quarters? Replacing the traditional quarter, those shiny new coins were all the rage as collectors waited impatiently for each state's commemorative coin to be released. The anticipation was intense at our house, too, especially by the shortest member of our family, five-year-old Noah.

My husband, Jeff, first introduced Noah to the new quarters, and it was an instant addiction. Each night after his dad got home from work, Noah followed Jeff to our bedroom and waited for him to empty his pockets and deposit his loose change on top of the dresser. Too short to see the pile, Noah stood on his tiptoes and pulled the coins down one at a time. He searched intently through his pile, dividing the coins into two categories: quarters and everything else. The "everything else" pile ended up back on the dresser, but the quarters remained clutched in his tiny, sometimes dirty, hands.

"Dad, which ones don't I have already?" he'd ask. Then the two of them would sit on the edge of the bed, carefully studying each shiny quarter, checking which ones had already made their way into Noah's commemorative coin book. As I was making dinner, I'd occasionally hear screams of delight coming from the bedroom as Noah discovered a new state quarter. Within seconds, he would be in the kitchen to show it to me, turning his treasure in every direction so the light could bounce off its shiny surface.

One night, I heard Noah rummaging through his toy box and dresser drawers.

"Mom!" he yelled from his top bunk. "Do you know where my money is?"

I told him I didn't and assured him that it would turn up somewhere. And it finally did . . . in the dryer!

Upon opening the dryer door, I jumped back when a half dozen extremely shiny quarters fell to the carpet.

"Hey, Noah!" I yelled. "I think I found what you're looking for."

He bounded down the stairs and came running to collect his lost treasures. "Good job, Mom, you found them!" He took the quarters in his small hands and carefully studied them. "Mom, all the fingerprints are gone, and they're better than before. Thanks!"

Noah's shiny coins had been perfect to him even before the dryer incident. When he had carefully chosen them from Jeff's dresser, he couldn't imagine they could be any better or any shinier until he saw them in an even better condition.

While watching him, I reflected upon my own life. How many days have I gone through the motions, happy with myself and the direction I'm moving, not even realizing that I could be a little better if I just made a few adjustments and cleaned things up a bit? On many days, I am shiny enough, but with a little work I could remove the dingy fingerprints and spruce up my attitude, my character, and my spirit.

SUDSY SUGGESTION

Keep a jar near your dryer to collect the occasional coins or even dollar bills that make their way through the laundering process. After a few months, total your findings and surprise your family with a night out for dinner. Your family won't miss an occasional quarter or dollar bill, but they will be thrilled that you turned their losses into a treat.

LOAD LIGHTENERS

The life span of a coin is 30 years, but if laundered many times, imagine how good that coin will look.

Paper money only lasts 18 months and much less when put through a heavy-duty spin cycle.

Washing and drying is actually the second of six steps in producing a coin.

Heidi Krumenauer is an author and freelancer, but spends her days as the political action director for a Fortune 400 insurance company. Heidi resides in Stoughton, WI.

IT ALL COMES OUT IN THE WASH

Melinda Hines

Chink, chink, chink . . . . As I rested in bed recently, I heard that telling sound coming from my laundry room. I knew, without even unwrapping myself from my warm, snuggly covers what was making the offensive noise. How in the world can such tiny pebbles make such a loud and annoying sound?

You may be wondering how rocks got into my dryer, unless, of course, you have an amateur archeologist in your family as I do. My daughter is an avid collector of rocks—all rocks. They don't have to be unique by the world's standards, such as bits of lava, chunks of granite, pieces of meteor rained down from the heavens, or even diamonds, a.k.a. a girl's best friend. Simple rocks, pebbles, and stones, randomly chosen along her path, are sufficient to satisfy her curiosity.

While I am a fan of my daughter's interest in the world around her, I have told her more times than I can count not to put her precious bits of God's earth in her pockets. Unfortunately, this day I missed a few of her valuables before I did the wash. I usually catch the remnants of her playtime as I empty her pockets and pre-treat for stains. But this day, I simply dumped her wet clothes from a plastic bag into our washing machine. (Clothes that were wet, by the way, because my little archeologist had been so wrapped up in her surroundings that she didn't quite make it to the bathroom in time. Geniuses are absent-minded, you know.)

These rocks that were permanently scratching the interior of my washing machine weren't just any rocks. According to Mackenzie, they were ones with great value.

"I was pretending the rocks were money," she informed

me. All I knew for sure is that she had accumulated a lot of "wealth." While transferring the clothes from the washer to the dryer, I had already disposed of more than a handful and thought they were all gone. As soon as the dryer was switched on, I discovered that I was wrong and was destined to listen to the cacophony of chinking until the clothes were dry.

Much as those tiny bits of playground gravel made their way into the dryer, hints of independence, stubbornness, and strong-will make themselves apparent in the lives of my children. Just when we think we have removed all the tiny flaws and imperfections in our children's character, a tantrum, a little white lie, or a full-blown rebellion forces us out of the warm, snuggly comfort of our false reality.

In the next load of laundry, I found a few chinking stragglers, and they reminded me that there will be more rocks in my future. Not just the laundry kind, either, but the tiny gravel bits of disappointment when my children do something I don't approve of, the pebbles of discontent as I question my value while doing yet another load of laundry, and bits of pumice rock as God refines my character as well as my children's. On the other hand, there will also be genuine gems of parental pride when my children make a good grade or win a game, crystals of faith when they choose Christ as their Savior, and precious jewels of hope as I pray they choose a godly spouse.

Experts say it takes thousands of years for rocks to change, during which time they are constantly being formed, worn down, and then formed again. In raising our children, however, we have but a few years to shape and mold them and foster their love for Christ. And then, in the end, it all comes out in the wash!

SUDSY SUGGESTIONS

Doing the laundry doesn't have to be drudgery! Creating an inviting work area may be just the motivation you need to keep up with the never-ending demands of your family's laundry. To set the mood, paint the walls a vibrant color and hang cheerful pictures or even old washboards. Keep the shelves well-stocked with all the essentials like detergent, bleach, stain remover, presoak, fabric softener, soap for hand-washables, starch, a zippered mesh bag for delicates, measuring cups, an old toothbrush for stubborn stains, hangers, and ironing supplies. To make the supplies look more appealing, pour the detergent in old-fashioned glass jars or place the supplies in a time-worn wash tub painted a bright color.

Melinda Hines is a Celebrate Moms' Team Member and lives in Texas.

EASTER MORNING

Dorothy Radmacher

It was Easter Sunday morning—a beautiful day to be alive, just as alive as my Savior was and still is! The Hallelujah Chorus was playing on the stereo in the living room, and we had hidden the Easter baskets for our two children, who would eagerly hunt for them when we returned from church.

I must boast just a little bit before I go on because I never washed clothes on Sunday. Even when dirty diapers piled up, they were obliged to wait until Monday. I never broke my "never wash on Sunday" rule until this particular Easter Sunday when our daughter was eight years old.

As I walked into the kitchen that morning, it was apparent that our dachshund, Zsa Zsa, had gotten sick and thrown up in her bed. What a mess! I had to make a quick decision—either break my "never wash on Sunday" record and clean up the stinky mess or leave it until Monday. The decision was easy. I went to the washing machine and turned on the water button to fill the machine so that when the water stopped running, all would be ready for the dog's bedding.

Well, not this time, because when I opened the machine to put in Zsa Zsa's blankets, I shrieked! Everybody in the family—even the dog—made a mad dash to the kitchen to see what my problem was. The lid was open on the washing machine, and everyone looked at the crazy mess inside. The water was brownish, with bits of a basket, green grass and pieces of foil candy wrappers floating in it. That's when our daughter, Heidi, remembered what she had done and started crying.

Heidi had wanted her mom and dad to hunt for baskets

that year. Knowing that I absolutely never washed on Sundays, she figured the washer and dryer were the perfect spots in which to stash our surprises. So, with a mixture of jellybeans, chocolate eggs, and a chocolate bunny, I had one grand mess to clean up early that Easter Sunday. Amazingly, we still made it to church on time that day. In fact, when my husband Roy and I got there, we quickly donned our choir robes and joined the choir for the processional hymn, "Jesus Christ Is Risen Today." We belted out the Hallelujah Chorus with more gusto than ever before.

LOAD LIGHTENER

Rejoice in the Lord always. I will say it again: Rejoice! (Philippians 4:4)

Dorothy Swanson Radmacher was born in 1923 and grew up in a parsonage. Mother of two and grandmother of four, this career homemaker is known for her cookies, her wit, and her infectious laughter.

ON A SOAPBOX

Marlene Barger

The colorful soapbox sitting in front of my neighbors' house caught my eye. "When did they start using that type of detergent?" I asked myself. It was the same kind that I used. That was unusual because the detergent was designed for washing machines, and I was probably the only person in the neighborhood who had one.

In the West African country of the Niger Republic, where I serve as a missionary, I live in one of seven small apartments that face a common, barren courtyard. In this yard, my neighbors wash their laundry by hand. To lighten the mothers' load of household tasks, children become responsible for washing their own school uniforms as soon as they start kindergarten.

"Diane," I asked my young African neighbor as she scrubbed one of her blouses, "when did you switch detergents?"

"I didn't," she replied. Diane tipped the soapbox to show me the locally-made blue powder inside. "I got your old box out of the trash and put my soap in it."

One man's trash being another man's treasure is more than a proverb in West Africa; it's a way of life. I remember the day when a neighbor marched into my living room with a scowl on her face. "You must do a better job of sorting your rubbish," she scolded. "The children have to dig through your coffee grounds to get to the good stuff."

"Please tell me what you consider the good stuff," I pleaded. "Where I come from, trash is trash and kids don't dig in it." With my kind neighbor's help, I learned to sort the good trash from the bad, and Diane didn't have to shake coffee grounds off her newfound treasures.

"Why did you put your laundry powder in my old box?" I asked.

"Because I want to be like you," she said.

Be like me? I didn't come to the Niger Republic to promote laundry detergent. I came to teach what it means to have a personal relationship with Jesus Christ. Is Diane doing other things to be like me? Do those things look like American culture or godly living?

Almost 2,000 years ago, another missionary, a man named Paul, wrote: The things you have learned and received and heard and seen in me, practice these things (Philippians 4:9a NAS).

"Lord," I prayed, "I have so many faults. Will I ever get to the point where I can, like Paul, invite others to imitate me?" Then I'm reminded that, even without an invitation, children like to observe and do what adults do. So every day I must seek God's help to live according to His guidelines, admit when I make mistakes, and ask for forgiveness.

The recycled carton at my neighbors' house hints that the most powerful lessons are not taught on a soapbox—they're taught by example.

SUDSY SUGGESTION

Bright sunshine in parts of Africa and many other places around the world can damage laundry on the clothesline. To minimize fading, turn clothing inside out before hanging it out to dry.

Marlene Barger first moved to the West African country of the Niger Republic in 1990. She currently directs a non-profit organization—Partnership Niger.

SECTION 3

Out of Sight, Out of Mind

LAUNDRY MISMATCH

Brenda Mayfield

While loading the washing machine, I sometimes noticed our sons' clean clothes in the dirty clothes hamper. And after finishing the last load and placing clean, folded shirts into my boys' dresser drawers, I would also discover dirty clothes shoved in with the clean ones.

"Oh, here we go again!" I said as I put down the laundry basket, which was still full of freshly laundered clothing. Instead of yanking out the soiled, stinky items from their drawers and hauling them to the hamper, I left them for the boys to deal with later—after my planned reprimand.

I went into the kitchen to heat leftovers for a quick supper before Wednesday night Bible study and then called the boys.

"Out of the sandbox! It's time to eat. Wash up!"

After dinner, I prodded my sons upstairs. "Hurry and change your clothes. It's time for church."

As I searched for my purse and books, my four-year-old returned, asking, "Mommy, what do I wear?" Thinking back to the dirty clothes in his drawer, I worried that he might choose them.

"There's a basket of clean clothes on your floor. Back upstairs. Hurry! Pick out a shirt and some pants from the basket. We'll meet you in the car." I shooed his older brother out the door. While we waited in the car, I arranged papers in my study book. As soon as I heard the rear car door shut, I started the engine.

My husband had driven straight from work in order to meet us at the church in time for music practice. When we arrived, the boys ran off to see their dad while I grabbed my things. I greeted a friend in the parking lot, then dashed to the prayer meeting. After the Bible study, many families met in the food court for dessert. As a woman in a red, chic dress spoke with me, I noticed her matching shoes and jewelry. My fingers felt the empty holes in my earlobes. Her son strutted toward us, and I admired his shiny, white pressed shirt. *How does she have the time?*

My thoughts were interrupted by the approaching voice of my youngest son—the one I had not looked at since sending him back upstairs to choose his clothes. "Here, Mommy," he said with confidence as he held out a drawing.

There he stood in pink and black striped pants and a green and blue flowered shirt. The clashing sight made me cringe. My face flushed, resembling the red in the dress of the woman whose jaw dropped as she stared at my son's attire.

How many people have looked twice at my boy tonight and wondered if his mom knows how to dress him? Remaining silent, I reached for the paper in his extended hand. At once, a huge smile stretched across his face—the smile that always warms me to the core. That night, there he stood clothed in pink and black stripes along with green and blue Hawaiian flowers, but beneath those flowers shone a heart full of joy. I finally replied, "That's my boy!" And the unique sight that started with a mismatch from a laundry basket ended with a colorful hug.

LAUNDRY'S LIFE LESSON

Happiness does not depend on perfection. Happiness is when you decide to see beyond the imperfections.

Brenda Mayfield is a freelance writer, teacher, and director of an international ministry, Prayer Support for Women. Brenda and her husband reside with their two sons in California.

DRESSING FOR SERVICE

Angie Peters

Be dressed ready for service ... (Luke 12:35).

Each laundry day, I used to dump the freshly washed and dried clothes onto our bed, fold them, and place them into neat stacks. Then, instead of putting them away, I would leave the pillars of towels, piles of pants, and rows of underwear on the bed like trophies for my husband and kids to see. The taller the towers, the prouder I was. How satisfying, knowing not only that I had handled such huge amounts of laundry in a day's time, but also that my efforts were not going unnoticed, thanks to my display. Who wouldn't notice five pairs of panties perched on your pillow when it's time to turn in? "See what I did!" those sweet-smelling piles seem to be triumphantly shouting for me and my oversized ego.

But after I was asked to write an article about raising kids with a heart for service, my spirit—as well as those stacks of laundry—came tumbling down. My reading and meditation about having a spirit of service taught me that, in trying to show everyone in my home what a servant I was, in no way whatsoever was I demonstrating a servant's spirit. Tooting my own horn was producing a melody that didn't sound very pleasant.

The world shouts, "Me first!" from the pages of books and magazines, and the plots of movies and TV shows spew strategies on how to come out ahead in whatever game it is we are playing. But God tells us we fare much better when we "dress for service" than when we "dress for success." Even though it clashes with the colors of popular opinion, I learned I need to outfit myself and my children with the attitude that service is sublime, not shameful.

So now, whenever I do laundry, I try to get those piles of clean clothes put away ASAP—before the others in my family come home from work and school. A "well done, good and faithful servant" from my heavenly Father will sound so much sweeter to my ears than a "look what I did" sounded to my husband and kids!

LAUNDRY'S LIFE LESSON

It's hard to even chat with a friend without using the words "I" and "me" a dozen times. Our children learn by watching us; may God help us—through our words and actions—demonstrate servanthood rather than selfishness, and transform our need for attention and commendation into a single-minded passion to please Him alone!

Angie Peters is a co-founder of Celebrate Moms and lives in Arkansas.

THE BASKET CASE

Barbara Lukow

Ever feel unappreciated, worn out, and convinced there just isn't enough time in the day? *If the kids would play quietly, I feel like I could get something done. No one realizes how much time it takes to be a mother. The work just keeps piling up, and I have no time to enjoy myself.* Those were my thoughts one afternoon as I did laundry and prepared dinner while watching my two youngsters play on the living room floor. Little did I know my tiny daughter was about to teach me an important lesson.

The potatoes were boiling, and the steak was frying. I had lowered the heat under the skillet and started a salad when the dryer timer sounded. As I headed down the hall toward the combination bath/laundry room, our 11-month-old daughter followed me. Because she was still a little unsteady on her feet, the little tyke chose to crawl in situations where speed was required. This was evidently one of those situations. She was right on my heels.

Opening the dryer door, I pulled out a load of clothes and dropped it into the nearby basket. Considering that the load was just underwear, and wanting to have dinner ready when my husband got home from work, I decided the folding could wait, and I quickly returned to the kitchen.

After turning the steak and draining the potatoes, I got busy finishing up the salad. During that time, our son, a mere 16 months older than his sister, played on the living room floor with his tractor. I smiled to myself. Finally, things were settling down a bit! While moving the highchair in preparation for setting the table, I was jolted into reality. The house was too quiet! Where was the baby? I scanned the living room and moved quickly toward the dryer, where

I'd seen her last. My heart pounded as I searched the bath and laundry areas in vain. I was leaving the room to continue my hunt when a quiet giggle caught my attention. Glancing back, I spied our precious daughter snuggled down in the basket of warm underwear. A pair of her Daddy's shorts hung on her head—her sparkling eyes peeking through one of the leg holes.

Amazed that she had climbed into the basket by herself and relieved to find her, I snatched her from her cozy sanctuary, hugging and kissing her. Laughing and pointing, she jabbered her desire to return to the basket. Pushing the worry of having to rewash the load to the back of my mind, I tucked her carefully into the soft underwear, grabbed up the basket and carried it to the living room, where she and her brother giggled and enjoyed their newly discovered playhouse until dinner was ready.

Over the years, I learned one lesson after another from my children. The most important lesson, however, began that day in the laundry room. God gives us children to love and cherish. Sometimes that job isn't easy. It takes lots of time and prayer, but He gives us enough time because we are human and make many mistakes. And He shows us how to pray because He knows once we recognize our humanness, we'll realize our need for help. Looking back now, I realize I should have internalized the lesson more quickly. Time slips away quickly, and prayer can easily be set aside in the busyness of life.

Now, 33 years later, our daughter is the mother of two lively preschoolers. Having learned at a much earlier age than I did to treasure each little snippet of life, she journals and photographs many of her children's prized sayings and actions, sharing them with her father and me. Because of her thoughtfulness and love, even though we live hours away from our grandsons, we are able to hold and cherish their precious "bits of life" in our hearts!

LAUNDRY'S LIFE LESSON
Time spent with your children is precious. Use it to make meaningful and loving memories. And remember, life is full of wrinkles. It takes time and prayer to iron them out!

Barbara Lukow has written stories, articles, and poetry for family and the classroom. A recently retired educator, she lives with her husband, Jim, on a small farm in northwest New Mexico.

Hanging Out, Hanging Up, and Hanging On

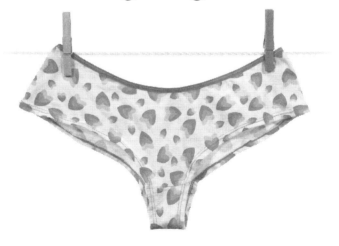

BRIDGING THE PANTY GAP

Kathy Howard

Nothing distinguishes teenage girls from their moms quite like their choice of undergarments. My daughters are all about fashion. The things they wear under their pants must be colorful and stylish. But for me, comfort is the name of the lingerie game. Panties must supply complete coverage, stay where you put them, and be versatile enough to wear under jeans or white slacks. We stand on opposite sides of the on-going underwear debate, with no agreement in sight.

This gap in panty philosophy was painfully illustrated one laundry day several years ago. At the time, both of my girls were in their mid-teens and I was ... well, I was considerably older than that. Now, as every woman knows, some articles of clothing are just too delicate for the dryer. And when there are three women in the house, those delicates often end up hanging from every available surface. So this particular wash day, the laundry room looked like Victoria's Secret after a two-for-one sale.

It just so happened that the girls had invited several church friends—of the male variety—over to watch a movie. Their mistake was in bringing the boys into the house through the garage instead of the front door. When you enter our home that way, you step directly into the laundry room. The girls screamed and hurried the guys out of the room as quickly as possible. However, the damage was already done. The fact that their guy friends had seen their panties was bad enough, but what really horrified them was that the boys had also seen their mother's.

After that, I determined to somehow bridge the panty gap. Giving up comfort was completely out of the question, but I was willing to break my rule about only buying white or beige. Surely some patterns and colors would open the door of lingerie communication with my daughters. So I bought a pink pair and one with a blue floral pattern.

My dear friend Susan even inspired me to shop on the edge of the wild side. One day, while we were having coffee together, a wayward bra strap revealed her fondness for animal prints. If Susan, a missionary and a conservative mother of two teenage boys, could cross the panty gap, then surely I could too! So the next time I was at the mall, I found a comfortable pair of leopard-print panties.

The next laundry day I proudly hung my pink, blue floral, and leopard print panties next to my daughters' far less comfortable undergarments. I thought surely this would bring an end to the strained silences I experienced whenever we happened to collect our clean, dry garments at the same time. But my hopes were dashed when my oldest daughter entered the laundry room. Apparently, my attempts to bring some youth and vitality into my lingerie wardrobe caused more embarrassment for her than had my original "granny" panties.

Fortunately, I have close relationships with both my daughters—relationships based on things far more important and lasting than what we wear. But I did learn two invaluable lessons during the "panty wars." Comfort truly is king (or queen), and the generational panty gap is better left uncrossed. Besides, in about 20 years I'm sure they'll find themselves on my side.

SUDSY SUGGESTION

Looking for a way to deal with all those unmentionables that are too delicate for the dryer? Many organization stores sell "lingerie dryers." Similar to a single coat hanger, the square bottom is covered with clips. You can hang more than a dozen bras and panties in a small space. In fact, the Container Store sells a stainless steel variety on its website at www.containerstore.com.

Kathy Howard is a Bible teacher, speaker, and mother of three. She serves on a church staff in Midland, Texas. Her Bible study, Before His Throne: Discovering the Wonder of Intimacy with a Holy God, *is due to be released in January 2008.*

SQUEAKY CLEAN

Sandra Stanford

"When are you going to replace that noisy dryer?" my neighbor asked half-teasingly. It's no secret to the neighborhood when the Stanfords are drying their clothes. Since I do laundry every day, they get a daily dose of the squeaking, creaking clamor of the ancient machine.

"I don't plan on replacing this dryer until it quits doing what it was designed to do—dry clothes." I smiled, thinking that it may be a little noisy, but the clothes still come out dry and smelling good. I can put up with a little noise. After all, I am a mom.

As I go through life, I have learned there are all kinds of noises clamoring for my attention, especially my children. Children make noises the moment they come into the world. Their cries are initially for food, a clean diaper, or just to be held. When they're older, they cry out for attention, and I want to be sure to meet this need so they don't turn elsewhere.

My teenage daughter, Anna Beth, often requests my attention. "Mom, will you watch this show with me?" she'll ask. Or, "I want to snuggle with you." She is crying out for "me" time. I realize it's her love language. That's a cry I hear that catches my ear.

"I'm coming!" I call out to her. "Get the blanket and the popcorn." As we snuggle and watch TV, we talk. She tells me about what's going on in her life, and it brings us close together.

Jonathan, my teenage son, makes noise, too. "When are we going out?" he'll ask. One of our favorite outings is to head to the local book store and read together. Or, we will read for an hour together, not talking much, just enjoying each other's company. The bottom line is that he wants me to give him some of my time. I admit . . . sometimes it's hard. There are times I just want to selfishly keep doing what I'm doing. I have to remind myself that my children need me.

One day I may decide to call a repairman to fix that noisy dryer. I won't call a plumber; I won't call the lawn company; I'll call Maytag. Likewise, I want my kids to call on me for questions they have in their lives. When they have questions about school, or wonder about life and death, I want to be the one they seek out for answers. I want to listen to them and spend time with them. I trust this will help us to develop a strong relationship. They will encounter difficult situations soon enough. Someone may offer them a cigarette or drugs, and I hope I will be the first person they tell when they come home from school.

Their peers will begin to make more noise in their lives than I do. When that happens, I want to be in tune with them to know when changes are taking place. I want to know when I need to step in because the noise has changed in my kids' lives and help them block out those wrong noises.

Who would believe that listening to a pesky, noisy dryer could give me life lessons? I've already done my couple of loads of laundry for today, but I know my dryer will be squeaking again tomorrow. My kids will probably be squeaking again, too. But I can put up with a little noise. After all, I am a mom.

LOAD LIGHTENER

Giving our children our time and listening ear will help develop strong relationships with them.

Sandra Stanford is a Celebrate Moms' Team Member and lives in Florida.

TINY LAUNDRY

Tonya Holter

Mothers hold their children's hands for a short while, but their hearts forever. —Unknown

I've never enjoyed doing the laundry more than when, towards the end of my first pregnancy, I started to wash all those baby clothes.

Sitting down to sort my yet-to-be-born son's first load of clothes, I had to reach around my swollen belly just to get to the laundry basket. I loved everything about those tiny clothes: the socks, so incredibly small, I was sure would get lost in the washing machine; the delicate little gowns that tied at the bottom to keep the baby's tiny feet inside; the soft, footed pajamas with their row of sturdy miniature snaps. I even savored the smell of the baby laundry detergent and fabric softener that saturated the air when I scooped all those little clothes out of the dryer.

A plethora of feelings flooded my heart as I handled each piece of clothing. There were the sweet fleece blankets that would swaddle my son, the terry towels with hoods I would use during bath time, and the burp cloths I would lay across my shoulder after nursing him. All those images came together to paint a vivid picture of reality: I was going to be a mother!

I let my mind run free, rehearsing scenarios of what motherhood would be like. As I realized that laundering this wee wardrobe was my first opportunity to actually do something for this baby I didn't even have in my arms yet, I was reminded of how Mary "treasured up all these things and pondered them in her heart" (Luke 2:19 NIV) when she was a new mom. Treasuring each moment of motherhood and

47

pondering all the hopes and dreams that come with each new life is what I started doing 17 years ago when I carried my first child—and I haven't stopped since.

As I think back to those baby-soft loads of tiny booties, bibs, and blankets, I have to laugh. With three kids now—ages 10, 13, and 17—the size of the loads and the size of the clothes have gotten much larger. I wish I could tell you that I still love sitting and sorting their clothes, but I can't; it's definitely a chore I don't always cherish! But, I do stop sometimes and think about what life will bring for each of my children. Even though they are bigger and the quantity of laundry they generate is huge, I treasure the time I have with them. I won't be doing their laundry forever.

LOAD LIGHTENER

Remember that behind every successful mom . . . is a basket of dirty laundry. —*Unknown*

Tonya Holter is a Celebrate Moms' Team Member and lives in Arkansas.

LAUNDRY ADJUSTMENT

Robbie Iobst

For me, the first year of marriage felt like one long appointment at the chiropractor. The awful cracking sound of "adjustments" filled our house daily. The loudest one came after the first time I did my husband's laundry.

I stood in the laundry room of our apartment complex staring at my husband's whitey-tighties. My eyes darted right and left wondering if anyone was watching me. No one was around. Still, embarrassment painted my face scarlet. *Silly,* I thought to myself. I had seen these briefs before. But to launder them felt weird.

After one load was completed, I felt more comfortable. Gratitude and joy replaced my awkwardness. These were my beloved's clothes. The simple assortment of polo shirts, long-sleeve button-downs, khaki pants, and jeans all belonged to my groom. It would be a delight to hang up his clothes, rub spot remover on his occasional stains, and sort his whites from his colors. Ahh, the rapture of doing my loved one's laundry!

When John came home, he kissed me hello, and we began to chat about our day. I almost heard bluebirds singing as we walked to the bedroom. I knew he would be thrilled when he saw my handiwork.

He opened the closet doors and said nothing. His silence surprised me. I figured that my act of kindness must have overwhelmed him.

"Robbie, what did you do to my clothes?" he finally said.

I was shocked by his accusatory tone.

"I did the laundry." Shouldn't he be ecstatic?

"I can tell." His voice was flat.

"What's wrong?" I asked.

"Everything."

In that moment, I wondered if we would make it. *How could he not be thankful? Where was the flattery I deserved?*

"John, what is it? A simple thank-you for taking care of your clothes would be nice."

"Robbie, don't you know me? Look at my closet."

It seemed fine to me. I shook my head. "What?"

"The polo shirts are mixed in with the long sleeved shirts. They aren't even facing the same way. The pants are mixed up, too, with the jeans by the khakis."

I sat down, defeated, and watched John "fix" his clothes. He arranged the polos so they all faced the same way and separated long sleeves from short sleeves and jeans from khakis.

Afterward, he sat next to me and grabbed my hand.

"I'm sorry. I overreacted, didn't I?"

I chuckled. "A little bit." But I squeezed his hand back. "Honey, I had no idea you were so particular." I didn't mean it as an insult but as a fact.

He took no offense. "Of course I am. I thought you knew."

We looked at each other and laughter erupted.

"I thought you'd be impressed."

"Oh, sweetie, thank you for doing my laundry."

"But never do it again?" I questioned.

"No, please do it. I love that you will do it," he assured me.

"But you want me to hang up your clothes . . . like . . . you just did?"

He paused. "If you don't mind. That's the way I like it."

The sound of a cracking spine pierced my ears. Another adjustment.

Hanging Out, Hanging Up, and Hanging On

Ten years later, my husband still likes his laundry hung just so. Our marriage has turned out to be built on a series of adjustments and acceptances, each one covered with commitment and love.

Although the rapture of doing my beloved's laundry is long gone, I still thank God for my John as I fold his underwear, which is no longer shocking to me at all. And I thank God again as I fold mini BVDs that belong to my eight-year-old son. My life is blessed by the two males God has given me as my family. He made them just like He wanted, from their mutual love of cars to the whitey-tighties they both wear.

The other day, my son informed me that he wanted all his colored T-shirts to be in one drawer and his white T-shirts in another.

I looked at John and rolled my eyes. He roared with laughter and said, "That's my boy."

Adjust, accept, and be grateful.

LOAD LIGHTENER

Let us be grateful to people who make us happy; they are the charming gardeners who make our souls blossom.
—Marcel Proust

Robbie Iobst is the blessed wife of John and proud mom of Noah. She is a freelance writer and speaker. Robbie lives in Centennial, Colorado.

NEVER THROW IN THE TOWEL

Bonnie Wheat

When I married my husband, Dwayne, almost 40 years ago, he had an oversized, slightly faded, red towel. When we merged our possessions into one 4 x 6 rental trailer to move 2,000 miles across county to our first home, the towel went with us. Although it didn't take long for me to fall in love with the comfy, worn towel, it was some time before I learned the tale that went with it.

Dwayne had received the red towel as a gift when he graduated from high school and had never used it until he took it to college with him the next fall. Several weeks into his first semester, Dwayne discovered that even though he had been sending his jeans and shirts out to be washed and ironed by a nice woman who made her living doing laundry for college students, he was out of clean socks and underwear. He had to make a visit to a strange new place called a laundromat.

Eager to get the job finished, Dwayne stuffed all his white clothes into a washer, poured in a generous amount of detergent, selected the hottest water temperature, and started pumping quarters into the money slots on the machine. By now, his new red towel had started to smell a little funny, so he decided to toss it into the washer, too.

When the machine had gone through all its cycles and spun to a stop, Dwayne hurried to retrieve his clothes and put them in an empty dryer before all the dryers were taken by someone else in the crowded laundry. But to his dismay, something terrible had happened. A look of horror came over his face as he pulled out one pink item after another. He could just see himself wearing a rose-colored T-shirt to his gym class or going into the shower room in blush-tinted underwear, and he didn't like that image.

While Dwayne was trying to decide what to do next, a motherly woman came over and helped him start the washer over again—this time, without the red towel. When the washer had filled and the water started swishing, she poured in some bleach. While they waited together for the "white" clothes to finish washing, she gave Dwayne a short lesson on laundry strategies.

I don't remember what finally became of the red towel. Perhaps it just dissolved in the laundry one day after years of being washed, or maybe it ended up in a rag bag somewhere. However, the tale of the red towel has always helped me remember some of life's greatest lessons. When we throw in the towel, things don't usually turn out the way we want them to. Further, throwing in the towel usually ends in humiliation because it means we gave up before we reached our goal. On the other hand, when we do make mistakes or do things we shouldn't, God can step in and, just as the bleach erased the lingering pink from Dwayne's T-shirts and underwear, He can erase the stains our sins have made on our own lives.

LOAD LIGHTENER

In the early days of boxing, a contestant's seconds would toss into the center of the ring the "sponge" with which they had wiped his face—a sign that their man could not continue, and they admitted defeat. The practice is continued today—except that a towel is substituted for the "sponge," hence the phrase, "throwing in the towel."[1]

Bonnie Wheat is a pastor's wife, retired teacher, and freelance writer from Big Spring, TX. She is the author of God Gives a Song: Walking with God through a Crisis.

DEAL OR NO DEAL?

Tonya Holter

"You're not going to believe this, but the washing machine is broken again."

These weren't the words my husband wanted to hear after a long day at work. And this wasn't the first time the washer had given us fits, but it was understandable because it was getting so old. This was the washer my aunt had given us—along with her dryer—when she bought a new pair of appliances for herself, when we first got married 17 years earlier.

After checking out the machine, my husband concluded that the cost of repair would exceed the value of the washer. In other words, it had finally bitten the dust, and we had no choice: It was time to go appliance shopping.

Now who doesn't get excited about the prospect of getting a new washer and dryer! I couldn't wait to pick out the newest, greatest machines on the market . . . that is, until we walked into the appliance store. As soon as we were accosted by a salesman showing off machine after machine, I became overwhelmed by all the choices. My head was whirling as fast as the spin cycle on the latest model. It was more than this modern-day mom could handle, even though I knew I had to make a decision soon because my laundry at home was piling up even as we shopped.

After seeing every make, model, and version on the sales floor, we started looking at the price list. Wow! Had I ever been wrong about how much we were going to have to fork out for our new state-of-the-art appliances.

I finally looked at my husband and said, "We have to leave now," and ran out of the store. On the drive home, I explained that not only had I been overwhelmed by all the choices, but that the price tags on the types of washers and dryers I wanted had nearly given me heart failure. The amount we were going to have to spend was enough to make a substantial investment into a college fund, for heaven's sake.

Meantime, we still didn't have a way to do laundry. What was a mom of three to do? I knew we had to decide something soon, and since I did the majority of the laundry, my husband was leaving the decision primarily up to me.

Regaining some clarity, I decided to pray about it. I felt a little silly, asking the God of the universe about a washer and dryer, but I knew God's Word promised that He would provide for my every need if I would just ask. He knew I wanted to be a good steward of our money, which meant getting the best deal.

I also did some comparison shopping. I realized that, of course, the root of the problem was that that the newest and greatest washers and dryers—the kind I had always wanted—were also the most expensive.

So, after much prayer and deliberation, I decided to go right back to the store resigned to buy only what we could afford. And that's just what I did, confidently asking the salesman to show me appliances that were more economical as well as efficient because we couldn't afford anything elite.

The salesman replied, "Well, I do have a washer and dryer that are marked down because they were returned yesterday after just one use. The woman who bought them said they had too many buttons to fool with, and she wanted an old-fashioned set again. Let me show you."

Much to my delight, it was love at first sight, everything a washer and dryer could be. The set came with a promise of laundering 105 towels in one load. (Well, not really, it was only 15—but I was so excited at the prospect of fewer loads per week it might as well have been over a hundred!).

When the salesman asked us, "Deal or no deal?" we bought the washer and dryer on the spot and had them home by the end of the day.

That episode taught me that God helps us even in the ordinary events of life. He really does give us the desires of our hearts if we delight in Him (Psalm 37:4).

I was just an ordinary mom trying to get her laundry done, and after offering Him my prayers asking for help and guidance, He generously provided not just what I needed, but what I wanted. He loves me that much.

And guess what, He loves you that much, too. He is big enough and kind enough to give me a great washer and dryer. What is your need?

LAUNDRY'S LIFE LESSONS

God really does care about everything we need, even if it seems trivial. Take some time to reflect on the needs in your life. Ask Him to supply your every need today.

And my God will meet all your needs according to his glorious riches in Christ Jesus (Philippians 4:19).

Tonya Holter is a Celebrate Moms' Team Member and lives in Arkansas.

MOUNTAIN SCALING

Kathy Pride

I stepped over the stained, dirty uniform strewn over my bathroom floor. It seemed like Matt's clothes always landed in a heap on the bathroom floor, crumpled and inside out, dropped haphazardly as he headed for a post-game soak in the tub. His socks were always inside out, his belt limply hung through one or two belt loops, and his jersey always had dirt stains from that last slide into home plate. And I was sure there were similar mountains of dirty laundry strewn all over his bedroom floor.

I stooped to gather Matt's clothes with yet another lecture about putting the dirty laundry in an appropriate place forming on my lips. Dirty laundry doesn't belong on the floor, I fumed. It belongs in a basket or a hamper—preferably hidden away in an inconspicuous corner to be gathered up all at one time and tossed in the washing machine where all the dirt, grit, and grime would be removed.

Stubborn stains might require an extra wash cycle or pre-treatment, but the dirt would come out. If necessary, I'd wash the uniform three times to get the stains out; the wash wouldn't go in the dryer until all the dirt came out first.

It reminded me of how I deal with family struggles or problems: I usually try to go back and fix them myself, repeating the same process over and over again—even if it isn't working. I make sure no one ever sees all the dirt and grass stains—I only display Clorox-bright whites and vibrant colors. No dirt there!

But at this time, the dirty laundry of family problems I was trying to keep out of sight was extremely personal: It was Matt's marijuana abuse. The troubles his drug abuse brought into our family not only included his substance abuse, but his belligerence, our lack of trust in him, and our family's disruption. I didn't have the energy to deal with this dirty pile any more than I had the energy to scale the mountain of laundry produced by our family day after day.

Then a thought came to me: What if I hung the laundry out to dry instead of secretly tossing it into the dryer? Freshness permeates clothes hung out to dry, and the clothes just seem to be cleaner when they air dry in a late spring breeze. If I hung out my struggles with Matt for others to see, would there be a freshness that would permeate my hurts? Would someone offer me a fresh approach, a gentle touch, or a soft word because I wasn't too ashamed to share my troubles? Could there be healing for me in airing my dirty laundry?

And could there be healing for someone else, too? Perhaps a friend or neighbor would be relieved to know that my laundry—like theirs and everyone else's—isn't perfectly white or clean.

I reflected on these thoughts as I stuffed yet another load of wash into the machine and hit pre-soak. I decided to give it a try; that day when I took the wash out to air dry, I hung Matt's out too.

LAUNDRY'S LIFE LESSON
Sharing our dirty laundry with others might help lighten our load.

Kathy Pride wears many different hats including mom, wife, friend, childbirth educator, and manager of scientific affairs for a medical education company.

LAUNDRY MUSE

Janet Hommel Mangas

Some people might consider me a laundry Nazi, but I like to think of myself simply as an efficient laundry CEO. When I'm doing the "last load of whites for the next week," I've been known to tackle playing children and yank them upside down by their ankles just to grab their dirty white socks. I've also been known to knock incessantly on the bathroom door, waiting for undergarments to be modestly tossed out into the hall by a shower-bound child—just to feed the last white load.

I don't play computer games, but I think getting all the dirty whites into the last load is my way of getting to the next level. Last week, I began to reminisce about how laundry has taken me to the next level by building my character.

1969—I learned a healthy fear from the wringer.

At 10 years old, I developed a healthy fear of Grandma Hommel's wringer washer. Before the spin-cycle days of wash machines, people used a wringer to squeeze the water from the wet laundry. The wringer, which had two mechanical rollers on a frame, was also called a "mangle" because that is what it did if you got your hands caught in it. My grandma would give her grandchildren anything, but was stern about keeping us away from the wringer when she was using it.

1974—I learned perseverance from hanging the sheets on the clothesline.

When I was a freshman in high school, I babysat an entire summer to save up enough money to buy myself a pair

59

of contacts. Hard contacts cost $187.50. My babysitting fee was 50¢ per hour. One summer day, while hanging the bed sheets out to dry on the clothesline, one of my new, hard-earned contacts popped out of my eye into the lush back-yard grass. As the clothes on the line flapped in the summer breeze, my hours of searching produced nothing. I roped off the area and called for back-up reinforcements. My little sister Jerri felt my pain, and even my younger brother Kevin came to my aid for a while. Mom and Dad spent a while searching, too. However, by the third day, the reinforcement team had vanished and suggested I get on with life. The worst pain came when Kevin was told to finish his chore of mowing the lawn. The crime-scene tape had to be removed and the MIA contact was now a cold case. Nevertheless, despite the naysayers and Kevin's smirk when he mowed over the area, I persevered. I found my contact later that night using a flashlight—three clothes-line drying days later.

1988—I learned contentment in a laundromat.

While single and in my late 20s, my hand-me-down, 30-year-old washer gave out, so I packed my laundry basket with the essentials and headed to the local laundromat. I have nothing but fond memories of hanging out there. Here are a few of my favorite things to do in a laundromat:

1) People watch: You can listen to the stories of people from all walks of life, with totally different experiences, while, ironically, doing the exact same thing—washing britches.

2) Read newspapers and magazines: It's amazing what a variety of reading materials there are and how much more interesting these media pieces are than watching your clothes tumble in a dryer.

3) Spend quality time with a loved one: One of the most

endearing qualities of one boyfriend (later-turned-husband) was that he actually volunteered to go to the laundromat with me. I would end up over-drying my clothes because we were laughing and our game of Uno wasn't finished.

2007—I learned to look forward to the unexpected.
For the past 17 years, I have found the strangest items when taking clothes out of our washer and dryer. I have found my husband's DayTimer, my daughter's homework, pens, markers, button collections, dirt clods from muddy boots, a fake mouse (not funny), toothbrushes, a fake pile of dog poo (funny), and lots of money.

In addition, just recently, I recovered my 10-year-old daughter's two special rocks. She came in panicked, asking if I had seen them. When I assured her that I had not thrown them into the yard but safely stored them on the laundry shelf, she sighed, explaining that they were her school friends' special make-up rocks—"we rub them together during recess to make colorful eye-shadow." It's comforting to know that she and her schoolmates now have clean eye-shadow.

2015—I will have more character building experiences.
In eight more years, I will be in my mid-50s and my laundry loads will be noticeably lighter. My three daughters will have their own laundry baskets. And although I will only be doing laundry for two, the chore will continue to build my character. Who knows, maybe for the first time my laundry will have no conservative whitey-tighties, but rather, matching "his-and-hers" purple polka-dot underwear? Now that would be character building!

LOAD LIGHTENER

"Don't worry; everything comes out in the wash, including the buttons." — Anonymous

Janet Hommel Mangas has done laundry at Purdue University while earning her B.S. degree, at IUPUI while doing graduate work in Journalism, and at Cincinnati Christian Seminary while earning her Masters in Ministry.

SECTION 5

Men in the Laundry Room

A LESSON IN HUMILITY

Wade Ivey

Why is it that I cannot seem to grasp the concept of how to wash and dry the laundry successfully? My wife has no trouble doing it. She quickly and effortlessly separates the mountain of clothes that our family of five heaps up, but I stay in a constant state of confusion whenever I try to help her with this chore. I used to think it was just separating colors, but then I found that it is also about types of fabric. You are supposed to add bleach to some, but never to others; some clothes are permanent press, others are not; some are to be washed in cold water, others in hot; then there's something about spin cycles and wash cycles.... Using the dryer is just as complicated. This load is for hot air—this one is for warm air—this one can't have any heat applied at all! Make sure you add the fabric softener to each load—except for the baby's clothes. Then I find that not all of the washed clothes are to go to the dryer; some must be hung up to dry! Which ones? How can you tell? Help!

My father used to try to teach me how to repair automobiles. He had the ability to know what was wrong with a car just by listening to it or by putting his hand on the car while it was running. He could also repair whatever was wrong and not have any leftover parts once the job was done. An old familiar glaze would come over my eyes whenever he would try to explain how this or that worked and how to repair it.

Over and over I've had that same foggy glaze when people with different abilities tried to explain their field of expertise to me. Time and again I've been amazed at how easy some things are for some people, while I struggle with it. It's not that I am an imbecile. I have an earned Ph.D., and there are certain things that I have a God-given ability to do with ease that people have applauded.

So, doing the laundry has become a lesson in humility for me. The problem with humility is that most of us are so self-centered that we see humility as the virtue of putting ourselves down. One day I was fortunate enough to have a young man named Jeremy explain to me the real meaning of humility. Jeremy has the wonderful ability to uncover and explain truths in such a way that encourages you instead of making you feel ignorant or stupid. He had discovered that humility did not mean putting yourself down—the real meaning of humility was lifting others up. Sure enough, when I looked it up, the dictionary defined humility as the quality of being respectful.

Now whenever I see the huge mound of laundry that needs cleaning, a big smile comes across my face instead of a frown. I think of my beloved wife Francine who has no problem multi-tasking laundry while preparing a message for a ladies' conference or writing another chapter for her next book. Every time I pass a mechanic's shop I think of those who, like my father, have the God-given ability to understand and repair engines. And so it is with all of life. We need one another, and each of us is gifted in our own unique way.

Humility is a great way to get rid of any false sense of pride, a great way to love and appreciate others, and a great way to help us see that everyone has an important part in God's plan. Remember that the next time you are trying to explain something to someone with glazed-over eyes.

LAUNDRY'S LIFE LESSONS
"Give me a laundry list, and I'll set it to music." —Gioacchini Antonio Rossini

"We should all do what, in the long run, gives us joy, even if it is only picking grapes or sorting laundry." —E.B. White

Dr. Wade Ivey and his wife Francine are the founders of WFI Empower Ministries. He is a pastor, musician, worship leader, speaker, and once-in-a-while laundry assistant. They live with their three children (Reagan, Peyton, and Gracen) in Mobile, Alabama.

TIDE OF EVENTS

Paula Hemingway

"Laundry shouldn't be that hard. I have a college degree, so I can figure this out." With that declaration, my 70-year-old dad opened the appliance, dumped the dirty clothes in with the detergent, slammed the door, set the dial to normal, and pressed start. Easy! Except for one problem: Dear Daddy had just loaded the dryer!

Dad's dabbling in domesticity didn't end with his creative new dry-cleaning method. He soon had another chance to prove himself master of home appliances when, once again, my mom had to take a rare trip out of town, leaving him home alone unsupervised. Deciding to cook his dinner, but needing guidance, my dad called a woman friend of the family.

"Now don't tell Carolyn that I asked you this, but how do you work the microwave?"

Daddy's failure in Homemaking 101 came naturally, by way of his disinterest and a lack of necessity. Having grown up on a farm as a male, his chores had included milking cows, chopping wood, and baling hay. His mother and sisters handled the indoor chores of cooking and cleaning. As common for the times, my father arrived at adulthood with few household skills and little desire or need to learn any. He provided well for his family by working long, hard hours and seizing financial opportunities that came along.

My mom, committed to the care of the home and raising us girls, created the strong, peaceful foundation my daddy needed in order to conquer the giants in his world. Through the years, Mom supported and provided for him by buying all his clothes and even picking out what he would wear each day. My sisters and I have often laughed about how

Dad still shakes his empty glass at the dinner table to not-so-subtly hint that he wants more tea. We were trained early to refill his glass, unaware that we were supposed to resent this churlish behavior. We didn't care; we loved our daddy! Dad certainly wouldn't win any laundry or culinary trophies, but life often twists and swerves like a washing machine out of balance, forcing improvement of our lackluster abilities. Such was the case with my dad, whose delay cycle into "women's work" was about to pick up speed.

Recently, Mom had knee replacement surgery, making it rather difficult for her to jump up at mealtimes to refill iced tea glasses. I wondered how Dad would handle household duties with Mom out of commission for six weeks. Who would pick out his clothes and wash, dry, and fold them? Who would cook the meals and clean up? Would Dad step up to the plate and do his duty, or would he fold under the pressure of having to distinguish whites from darks, properly care for delicates, and maintain a well-groomed lint trap?

When visiting my parents during Mom's convalescence, I found the house amazingly tidy and clean, so I secretly searched for dirty dishes, laundry piles, and grime. I came up as empty as a vending machine at the local laundromat. Had my dad paid for a maid, cook, and butler? Or had he performed this housekeeping miracle himself? All weekend I watched in astonishment as this man, who had mostly been waited on his whole life by his wife and four daughters, became my mom's caretaker, physical therapist, and encourager.

Late one night, my sister placed some dishes on the kitchen counter, commenting that she would take care of them the next morning. Dad would have none of that. "These need to be cleaned up now," he pronounced with all the authority of an experienced household executive.

68

Men In the Laundry Room

At one point, though, Dad related that he was a little stressed with all the household responsibilities, to which I replied, "How would you like to also have four kids running around who need attention and cause more work?" He could barely fathom that, but of course realized Mom had done it quite well for many years. Now, too, the microwave hummed at his touch, the correct appliance (the one with a tub, agitator, and water) swished the clothes, and the machine with the waterless drum tumbled wet articles as it blasted hot air to dry them. Amazing.

That night as I slid between the crisp, clean sheets and laid my smiling face on the fresh pillow, I thanked God for my parents' renewed appreciation for each other—my dad realizing how much work Mom does to keep the home running smoothly, and Mom learning that Dad loves and cares for her enough to master new skills and work hard for her welfare.

How fortunate I am to have these parents of mine—married 56 years—still showing me what a great marriage is all about.

LAUNDRY'S LIFE LESSON
Loving and serving those closest to us brings honor to God. How can you do that today?

Paula Hemingway is a mother of six from Keller, Texas. By her estimates, she's washed 11,648 loads of laundry during her 32-year marriage to husband Mark.

DO I HAVE TO FOLD IT, TOO?

Steven Brown

I swung open the windows and drank in the fresh air. It was 9:30 on Saturday morning, two weeks after our wedding. The evening before, I had brought home fresh flowers for my new bride. The scent of the flowers and the aroma of coffee filled the room. We savored our chocolate croissants as we enjoyed each other's company.

"Honey, we should decide how to divide up the chores." Even though it still sounded funny to me when I called her "honey," it felt quite natural.

"What chore do you dislike the most?" she asked.

"I really don't like to clean the bathroom. What about you?"

"I don't mind cleaning the bathroom. It doesn't take very long. But I hate doing the laundry."

"I don't mind the laundry at all. It takes a while, but you can do other things while the machines are running. I think we have a deal."

An hour later, she was assembling the cleaning solutions and brushes, and I was separating whites, lights, and darks. I loaded up the clothes and started the machines in the laundry room upstairs from our apartment. Half an hour later, when I put the clothes in the dryer and came back to the apartment, my wife was sitting down to another cup of coffee, having finished cleaning the bathroom.

"I'm going to enjoy this! I'm all done with the bathroom, and now I get to watch you finish the laundry."

"I'll enjoy it, too. I didn't have to clean the bathroom, and I get to drink coffee with you while I wait on the laundry."

When I came back down with the dry underwear, I

poured it out in a pile on the floor. I put her laundry basket on the left, and mine on the right.

"Mine, yours, mine, mine, yours, yours, yours, mine, yours . . . ."

She got up to go to the bathroom while I finished sorting. By the time she came back, I had already dumped my underwear in my dresser drawer. I handed her the other basket.

"Here's your underwear."

"But honey, it isn't folded. I thought you were going to fold it."

"Fold it? I never fold underwear. I always just dump it in the drawer."

"But I always fold it!"

I looked at her basket. The underwear was a jumbled mess. Some of the panties were tangled and twisted together. I picked up a clump of undergarments and smiled as I held them up.

"Are your panties in a wad?"

She chased me around the apartment and threw other wads of panties at me until I grabbed her and kissed her.

In a new family, we have a chance to learn from each other. The way I do something may not be the only right way. Sometimes, my spouse, or even my children, will teach me a way of doing things that reflects a different set of priorities. I will grow more as a person if I am open to new ideas. I may need to fold my wife's panties (or at least untangle them) if for no other reason than because it is important to her. On the other hand, a few years later, when she was a stay-at-home mom and we had three children in diapers at the same time, there were a few weeks when she took the underwear straight from dryer to drawer . . . without any folding.

LAUNDRY'S LIFE LESSONS

There are at least three important lessons in this story: Sometimes what one person hears is not what the other person means. 1) We have to talk through the details to be sure we understand each other. 2) When there is such a misunderstanding, we have to renegotiate. 3) While it is usually important to strive for excellence in all that we do, sometimes other goals are more important. If it lets me read one more story to little Andrew, for example, sometimes I should put the underwear in the drawers still wadded up.

LOAD LIGHTENER

Did you know that in the Bible, at the end of Luke 10, Jesus actually commends a woman for not doing housework so she can spend time listening to Him? I shouldn't use family time as an excuse to shirk my genuine responsibilities, but I don't need to let laundry rule my life either.

Dr. Steven Brown lives in Midland, Texas, with his wife of 21 years and three children. His new book, Navigating the Medical Maze: A Practical Guide, *is due out in late 2007.*

LAUNDRY MAN TO THE RESCUE

Shannon Jacobyansky

There is no stain he can't remove, no mountain of dirty clothes he can't surmount. His athletic thighs bulge with muscle tone as he lifts the half-ton of laundry, and his biceps hit the ceiling as he reaches for the super-value-sized box of detergent. His well-defined calf muscles ripple as he carries the folded clothes up the stairs.

It's a bird . . . it's a plane . . . NO! . . . It's Laundry Man!

If superhero status were awarded for expertise in the laundry room, his name would be my husband, a.k.a. Laundry Man. He has done the deed most people detest ever since we've been married—15 years to be exact. Laundering clothes for our family of five never frustrates him, and he never complains. Some superheroes' credo is "Crime never pays"; my husband's motto is, "If you just do a couple of loads every day, the task is never overwhelming."

I did not take his advice once when he was away on a business trip. It was Thursday, and I hadn't done one stitch of laundry all week. I quickly sorted the clothes in the morning and figured I had all day to catch up. I put a load in and went upstairs to do other cleaning. I returned to the laundry room about 30 minutes later only to find something was wrong with the washing machine. The clothes were sitting in a tub full of water and had never gone through the spin cycle. Oh no! Where is Laundry Man when you need him?

I hadn't a clue what to do. In anguish, I cried out for help, hoping Laundry Man would appear from a phone booth dressed to help the damsel in distress. (Actually, I picked up the phone and called my husband.)

"What's wrong with the washer?" I asked my superhero.

"Just bang it real hard on the right side with your hand. If you hit the correct spot it will start back up again," he answered.

After many futile attempts to find the right spot, I eventually hit it because the washer started running where it had left off. I reached for the blue painter's tape and marked the spot with a big "X." Several loads and a tired, bruised hand later, I looked in dismay at all the laundry left to do. Oh, why hadn't I listened to Laundry Man's advice and done a little each day?

I did finish the daunting task before my husband returned home the next day, but not without learning some good lessons I also shared with my children. First: Don't put off until tomorrow the things you can do today; procrastination only causes worry to one's heart. The unfinished business follows you around like a cloud. And second: Never take for granted what others do for you—in the big and the small stuff alike—to help make your life a little easier.

LOAD LIGHTENERS

Always choose the clothes you're going to wear that day by whatever garments would bring you closest to a full load.

Make everyone in the family use his or her bath towel twice to save at least one load of laundry each week.

Shannon Jacobyansky was born and raised in the rolling hills of western Pennsylvania and currently resides in Chesterton, Indiana, with her husband Bill and their three children.

SECTION 6

It's a Family Affair... Or, Maybe Not?

BLACK (SOCK) HOLE

Sandy McKeown

"Where are my black dress socks?" my husband calls out from the bedroom.

"Did you check the laundry room?" I answer from the kitchen.

"I looked, they're not there . . . ."

It's one of those conversations we've repeated many times throughout our 28 years of marriage. With four growing boys needing black dress socks for their jobs, various band performances, and occasional formal events, finding a pair of clean black dress socks in our house is like finding gold.

It hasn't been easy keeping track of everyone's laundry in a large family, but our system has morphed through the years into one that works for us—at least, most of the time.

First, I have always tried to have a regular wash day, and I remind each family member to get his dirty clothes to the laundry room by then. This puts less of the laundry-gathering burden on one person (me)—meaning I don't have to hunt down all the items needing washing.

Second, with four boys, there are naturally a lot of hand-me-downs. Our system is simple: on the tag of each garment for our oldest son is one 'x' that means it is his. Once our first son can no longer wear the garment, the tag receives another permanent 'x' alongside the first one, which signifies it now belongs to the second son's clothing pile. This process eliminates writing names on tags that are no longer pertinent once they outgrow the item.

Third, the boys are pretty happy that they never have to wear hand-me-down socks and underwear. To keep track of the jumble of white t-shirts, briefs, and tube socks, I buy each of my sons different brands. For example, one gets Nike socks with Hanes underwear; another gets specific store-brand socks with Jockey underwear, and so on. (This not only helps us sort, fold, and distribute the items to their correct owners, but it also helps me police their household habits. When a forgetful son leaves his pair of dirty socks in the middle of the living room floor, I can tell right away whose they are!)

Fourth, using masking tape, I marked off six equal sections on the surface of a 3-by-6-foot folding table. Each family member has a section on the table for folded clothes. When the kids come in the laundry room looking for clean clothes, they don't have to guess which piles are theirs.

And, finally, when the stacks are dangerously close to tipping over in the laundry room, I call for an impromptu "laundry-putting-away party" and all family members are invited—no "regrets" are allowed!

Our system works pretty well, except for those elusive black socks. I still don't know where they all end up. We bought five new pairs for my husband and sons to wear to my oldest son's wedding, and even after that, my husband is still having trouble finding a pair. Maybe that's where we get those black holes in space—it's where all the black dress socks end up!

SUDSY SUGGESTION

Buy each of your children different brands of socks; that way, it's easier to spot who they belong to.

Sandy McKeown is a Celebrate Moms' Team Member and lives in Iowa.

LAUNDRY ROOM SECRETS

Kathy Firkins

Only once during the last seven years as a professional organizer have I been asked to help organize a laundry room. Laundry rooms, by definition, are small nooks that only house the washer and the dryer. Rarely—because of their size and function—do they become a place for colossal clutter.

Whatever trivial or insignificant emphasis we place on the laundry room as a décor-inspired masterpiece, I think it is worth a little more effort to make this mundane and very important chore more pleasant. Here are my best tips for you from a practical standpoint.

Inspire Yourself

Laundry shall not be done in pain. This chore, much like washing dishes, should not inflict suffering on the laborer. Kitchen sinks are often set near a window because the chore is so boring. Enjoying the outside view and perhaps seeing something we would rather be doing help motivate us to get it done. Doing the laundry should be treated in the same way. Consider these options:

• Paint your laundry room a daring and inspirational shade of pink or consider splashing on a nice aqua blue (or whatever your favorite color is).

• Add some of your own artwork such as a brown-and-white cow print.

• Hang something on the walls to spruce up the view. Display artwork that inspires you. Or string up a clothesline decorated with all those mismatched socks. (Maybe you'll eventually find their mates!)

It's a Family Affair . . . Or, Maybe Not?

Prepare Yourself

A well-stocked laundry room enables you to be prepared for any stain or laundry situation. Make sure you have the following supplies on hand:

- Basin or tub for soaking and hand washing.
- Baskets or hampers for sorting. (I like to place the next load to be washed on top of the washer so that it gets it off the floor in my tiny laundry room and makes me feel like I am accomplishing a bit more.)
- Hangers and hanging rack.
- A timer to take with you around the house. This will let you know right away when it's time to change the loads.
- Laundry detergent, bleach, stain treater, small toothbrush (for those hard to reach stains), and fabric softener.
- Iron and ironing board.

Training Required

Kids as young as three should be helping with the laundry; by age 10 or 12 at the very latest, they should be responsible for washing, drying, and putting away their own clothes. Remember, this isn't being mean; it is equipping them to be productive, self-sustaining adults. Do you really want your kids to drop off their smelly laundry for you to do when they are adults?

Start Young and Start Slow

- 3 to 5-year-olds should be able to place their neatly folded clothes in the correct drawers with your guidance.
- 6 to 7-year-olds should be able to fold towels and put them away, even if that means using a small step stool.
- 8 to 11-year-olds can learn to work the washer and dryer, as well as fold their own clothes. While they are learning, you may want to post "Laundry Policy and Procedures" as a reminder.

• By age 12, they should be totally self-sufficient in the laundry room. This is time to make them completely responsible for doing their own laundry. It may help to schedule certain days for each child to do his or her laundry, and each child should have only about two or three loads a week. Make a paper magnet your child can place on the washer and dryer identifying their clothes. You may also want to write down the schedule and post it in the laundry room.

Organize Yourself

Use a spring-loaded clothes rod stretched across a doorframe or in between two wall cabinets to hang your wet clothes on to dry.

A wall-mounted iron rack keeps the iron and ironing board off the floor and out from under your feet.

Rolling carts are great for transporting clothes, hanging up wet clothes, or hanging clothes just removed from the dryer. Smaller carts can be used to store laundry detergents, bleach, and fabric softener right where you use them.

Several good hampers are a laundry laborer's best friend. Use them to separate laundry, carry clean clothes to their destination, or even to turn upside down and sit on for a nice little cry.

Designate a mesh bag in the laundry room for dry-clean-only pieces. Set a specific schedule—for example, the 1st and 15th of each month—to drop off dry cleaning. (And don't forget to pick it up!)

Place a bowl for catching all your laundry finds, such as money, lip balm, gum, and crayons before they get washed and dried. Use the money you collect to make a coffee run—quick, before anyone notices!

It's a Family Affair . . . Or, Maybe Not?

SUDSY SUGGESTIONS

Don't let clean laundry lie around in laundry baskets. Boy, do they wrinkle up fast! Put hanging items on hangers right away.

Get rid of things you or your children no longer wear. Clean out your drawers and closet during spring and fall. This will make sure you have enough room in your closets and drawers for the clothes you enjoy wearing.

Add a dry towel to the dryer with a load of wet clothes. They will dry faster.

Throw a damp washcloth in the dryer along with your wrinkled clothes; this should pull out all the wrinkles. Using a soaking wet washcloth will only leave your clothes with wet spots!

Close zippers, snaps, and hooks to prevent snagging and tangling.

Kathy Firkins is a Celebrate Moms' Team Member and lives in Texas.

MATES FOR LIFE

Melissa Howell

The most important thing she'd learned over the years was that there was no way to be a perfect mother and a million ways to be a good one. —Jill Churchill

Mom's face was scrunched and filled with confusion.

"What's that?" she asked, pointing to the big yellow bucket in the corner of my living room.

I was in the middle of giving her a quick run-through of the house and its day-to-day operations before leaving her with my kids for a week while I attended a writers' conference.

"Oh, I was getting to that," I stated matter-of-factly. "It's The Yellow Tub. I don't match socks; I just throw them in there, and we fetch them as we need them."

At one time or another, most socks in our house usually end up spending time in this centrally located "singles hangout." Some of the crews, tubes, and anklets destined to remain single forever inch their way to the bottom of the tub, forcing the owner to file a missing sock report: "Mom, I can't find my sock!" The more adventurous socks, however, remain near the top of the tub, hoping to be easily accessed should a perfect match arrive on the scene.

The matchmaking system varies, depending on who's doing the sorting. For example, my husband Gary takes great care to choose the perfect mate for each sock. A vigilant inspector, he pays close attention to colors, seams, sizes, and special markings—anything that might help him arrange a suitable partnership. His painstaking attempt to pair up the socks of our six family members generally ends, however, with a frustrated announcement: "I think we should throw all these out and start over."

Gary is the exception in our family. The rest of us choose socks' mates without such thought and consideration—we put together "blind dates" of the worst sorts.

Take my oldest child, Ken. He may pair Mr. Blue Tube Sock with Miss Red Ankle Sock—a seemingly dreadful duo—but, to Ken's thinking, the right pants and shoes might present this relationship with opportunities unavailable to socks paired by another matchmaker.

Breana, my nine-year-old, likes to join her "holey" socks with "un-holey" partners. When she does this, we all anxiously watch to see which sock—the saint or the sinner—will cross over to the other side.

As it turns out, the singles scene isn't for 14-year-old Elizabeth at all. She makes sure her socks enter into arranged marriages, never allowing them to be tossed into the questionable population of The Yellow Tub. From the moment she peels her socks from her manicured feet, she pierces them and links them together with a safety pin—a Cupid's arrow, of sorts, ensuring that they will enter and exit the laundering cycle with their mate for life.

Watching how my husband and children handle their matchmaking duties has taught me that there are indeed many ways to accomplish—with success—a single task. From carefree Ken to organized Elizabeth, they all get the job done. They just use different tactics and, most days, each of us leaves the house with a sock on each foot.

It's much the same with mothering. When I'm tempted to compare the way I run my home and care for my kids to another mom's parenting style, I have to remind myself that a good mother is defined in a million different ways, and a perfect one does not exist—just as Jill Churchill says in the quote above.

One day, The Yellow Tub will be empty of our kids' socks. The children will be grown, and they'll be developing sock-mating systems for their own families. When that day comes, I hope I can look back on these days of mothering with peace and confidence, knowing that while I wasn't perfect, at the very least, I was a good mom . . . who did it the best way I knew how. I can live with that!

LOAD LIGHTENER
Did you know the first Thursday in January is National Clashing Clothes Day? Create a new family tradition and start celebrating this national holiday as a reminder to lighten up and not take things so seriously. Check out Silvana Clark's book, *Every Day a Holiday*, for more wacky ideas.

Melissa Howell is a co-founder of Celebrate Moms and lives in Alabama.

MULTIPLIED LAUNDRY DUTY

Karen Whiting

The hurricane arrived with a bang as the French doors blew open. Becky, my oldest at nearly 16, slammed them shut and pushed against them with all her might as I tied the door handles together. As an added reinforcement, we piled furniture against the doors. Glancing out the window, I noticed that the powerful winds forced the huge Gumbo-limbo trees in the park to bend in half. Strong limbs were snapping off like twigs.

"Let's get out of here! Run!" I yelled. Becky raced up stairs in front of me to the master bedroom closet. I pressed my hands into fists and suppressed yelling out to God, trying to stay calm for my children's sake.

Winds shook the house and sounds of crashing glass filled the air as I dashed into the closet and dropped onto the floor. It had no windows, plenty of space, and a second story location. At least we would not end up crushed if the house collapsed!

When Hurricane Andrew finally left, it had destroyed half our home and also left us temporarily powerless. As a mother of five, I understand the dreaded multiplying factors involved with delayed laundry. Due to Andrew, we had an incredible mountain of clothes that would rival a garbage dump. But we couldn't attend to that mountain right away. We had debris to clean up, soaked carpets to cut into pieces and drag out of the house, and a living room to bail. We labored in the midst of Miami's heat and humidity as a result of no air-conditioning, and the stench grew unbearable. Imagine three-dozen pairs of dirty socks in a few days as just one part of the odor. I sprayed deodorizers and per-fumes frequently to little avail.

Thankfully, the electric company restored our power five days after the hurricane. The washer immediately went into full swing, load after load. We first washed things already starting to mildew from the rooms that had been totaled. I praised God for my washing machine and electricity that night. We had barely caught up on our wash when we attended church and our phone service returned. I discovered that many or our friends' homes remained powerless. I knew the horror of no electricity in high humidity and heat so I quickly volunteered to wash clothes for them. Thankfully, the moms, continuing well-practiced habits, checked pockets and sorted darks from lights before dropping off their wash.

One mother, Sherry, came with her two children and stayed with us for a few days because she suffered from MS and needed air-conditioning. Our children shifted around to fit our family into two bedrooms so we could let her family have the third undamaged bedroom. Sherry folded and sorted clothes for other families with me as we talked and shared our hurricane experiences.

Our washer and dryer stayed busy for the next three weeks. I prayed that the nearly 20-year-old machines would not go on strike by breaking down to protest so much use. They eventually survived the endless washing and drying for other families. We squeezed in our own wash, too, and after friends had power restored, we gave our machines two days off for good behavior.

My husband and children helped with the extra washing and folding, usually saying, "I'll fold so you can cook. I'm starving." They plopped the loads from washer to dryer and into baskets for folding.

Sometimes the Lord calls us to a ministry that is less than glamorous. Doing laundry for dozens of people had never been in my plans. I thought washing thousands of socks, undies, shirts, and pants for seven people filled my days enough. But when disaster strikes and our lives change, so do our hearts. With a two-year-old at home, I couldn't easily help out at the homeless shelters. I couldn't get out and help with other people's homes when I had to be at my home to let workmen in and supervise repairs. I couldn't pick up pieces of roof tiles that littered the streets, cut up damaged trees, or help others bail out their homes. So, I joyfully washed clothes. As others faced more powerless days, I had restored power to help them. I realized that I am never powerless to help others when I am plugged in to God's power. And I prayed for each person as I washed his or her clothes.

The smiles and hugs from appreciative friends let me know how much they appreciated our efforts. When I visit my grandchildren, I also try to give their moms time off by doing laundry for them. It's a powerful way to show both my love and Jesus' too.

SUDSY SUGGESTION

If a neighbor has a new baby, or is facing a difficult situation, offer to wash clothes for them. Pray for the family while doing their laundry. Return the clothes folded with a cheerful note on top.

Karen H. Whiting is a Celebrate Moms' Team Member and lives in Maryland.

LAUNDRY CHATS

Sue Ferguson

"Mom, I've gotta go; love you!"

"Okay, I love you, too! Bye!"

Pushing the "End" button on my phone, I picked up the stack of towels I'd folded while chatting. My emotions matched the cheerfulness of the freshly painted bathroom as I placed the towels on the shelf and realized I've been doing laundry with my three children for nearly three decades. Never mind the fact that they are in Arkansas, Oklahoma, and California now, and I'm in Georgia; we still routinely do laundry together.

When the personalized ring tone identifies one of my kids as the caller, I pick up the phone and naturally move toward the laundry basket with socks to match or clean clothes to fold. Sometimes I simply wipe off the top of the washer and dryer or reach for a handful of hanging clothes to carry upstairs to the closet. Occasionally, I push "Speaker" and lay the phone on my ironing board as I press my husband's shirts while I connect with my children's lives. I love doing laundry with them.

A spontaneous smile crept across my face that day as I placed the towels on the shelf and comfortably followed the mental image that transported me back 25 years. Nathan, my blond, curly haired 2-year-old, was hanging clothes on the wooden drying rack I'd temporarily set up in the living room of our first little house. Eager to preserve that precious moment, I rushed to get my camera. It didn't matter that he was unfolding and hanging dry clothes from my just-completed stack. He was my helper, and we were doing the laundry together.

Traveling forward a bit in my journey back in time, I saw

two grade-schoolers and a bright-eyed preschooler folding clothes taken from the mounds piled high on my smoothly made bed. We sang gleefully as we worked together. Each time Nathan walked away to deliver a pile to another room, I broke out in a silly little dance. With shocked and delighted expressions, Karissa and Audri laughed hysterically, and my son curiously turned around to see nothing but my instant return to methodical folding. We girls giggled until our sides ached, and Nathan, not certain why, smiled good-naturedly anyway.

Laundry, like life, teeters back and forth between routine fun and overwhelming drudgery. Often, when the children were young, two laundry baskets overflowed with unmatched socks, and I desperately searched for someone to delegate the task to, even if it meant hiring help. Many times my children laboriously laid lonely socks on the living room floor, searching intently for look-a-like partners. Their side-by-side laundry chats were building lifelong bonds. A few nickels were cheap therapy for their weary mom and a generous compensation for those with no bills. Once again, our task was completed with teamwork.

The children grew and continued to help; life got busier. In high school, they faced a new reality—Mom needed everyone to do his or her own laundry, and there were no paychecks. When the skills were learned, the job ceased to be a group activity. There was still cooperation and communication, even some cheering from the sidelines, but each player, most often, played alone.

Now my laundry mounds look more like molehills than mountains. The few socks are easily matched, and I rarely bother with a basket. But, once again, I treasure doing the laundry with my children, typically by phone. Together we discuss preventing and treating life's stains, smoothing out wrinkles in relationships, and our jubilation over well-completed tasks. After saying good-bye, thankful for decades of laundry chats, I fold my grown children's lives in prayer.

LAUNDRY'S LIFE LESSON

Unfortunately, most people spend more time planning an annual vacation than considering the memories made daily, or at least weekly, doing laundry. Ponder the impact of seizing brief, teachable moments and routine opportunities for chatting, fun, and laughter. Purpose and plan for laundry to be one of the most influential activities you do with your children.

Sue Ferguson admits that life has taken this homemaker at heart through the daily adventures of marriage and motherhood.

It's a Family Affair . . . Or, Maybe Not?

A SINGLE LAUNDRY BASKET

Marilyn Nutter

When my daughters were in college, they often brought friends home to hang out, watch a movie, and eat a home-cooked meal. Occasionally, the girls would do a load of laundry. It amazed me that they could do all their laundry in one load; I rarely saw them do two.

My laundry room, on the other hand, houses several baskets holding specific loads of laundry: whites, darks, permanent press, garments to be washed separately, and jeans. College students don't have time for that kind of organization. Except for jeans, everything goes in at once. I tried to convince them that doing their laundry that way shortens the life of their clothing, but they insisted they don't have the time to devote to many loads. Aside from laundry, college students have many tasks to juggle and not enough time in which to juggle them.

Moms face the same dilemma. A day limited to 24 hours calls for mothers to perform quite a balancing act. Starting with breakfast, a mom's day might include work outside the home, baking cookies for a class party, chauffeuring children to activities, vacuuming carpets, and returning home to prepare dinner. After-dinner activities might include cleaning up, helping with homework, and packing the kids' lunches for school the next day. She might even throw in a load of laundry before falling into bed and waking up the next morning, only to repeat the cycle the following day. Time for Mom's self-care gets lost in the shuffle and is often dumped into the laundry baskets along with assorted colors and fabrics.

But in order to take care of others well, it's important for moms to know we need to take care of ourselves. Whether it's taking a few minutes with a cup of tea and a bit of quiet, reading a chapter in a good book, polishing our nails, having lunch with a friend, or engaging in 20 minutes of exercise, moms need to create a laundry basket labeled: "Handle separately—self-care." Prioritizing specific tasks, budgeting time, and including pampering moments are part of a separate load that mothers should include in their weekly routine.

Sorting laundry and washing fabrics according to the instructions are part of responsible clothing care. Somehow, when I sort through my priorities and set aside time for myself, I know that I am being responsible too. By caring for myself, I am also caring for my family. When I choose "Handle separately—self-care," there is less wear on my physical, emotional, and spiritual fabric, and my life is extended. At least it feels that way.

SUDSY SUGGESTIONS

Children can learn to sort laundry at an early age. Keeping a divided hamper in a child's room teaches sorting skills, clothing care, and personal responsibility.

Moms can sort out their days and schedule personal pampering moments by using a daily planner, taking advantage of voice mail, and delegating some jobs to family members. The Internet and bookstores offer loads of resources to improve personal time management and home organization.

Marilyn Nutter and her husband of 37 years live in western Pennsylvania. Marilyn is the author of Dressed up Moms' Devotions to Go *(2006) and* Tea Lovers' Devotions to Go *(2007).*

TAKE THESE SOCKS AND STUFF 'EM!

Kathy Firkins

Kaiti, our oldest child, is now well-mannered, compliant, and helpful—an absolute joy. However, like most pre-teens, she began her transition into adulthood by testing the limits of respect and power.

I started to notice her sharper-than-usual tongue in the seventh grade, when she began to use a harsh tone of voice when she spoke. It was a tone I was all too familiar with, as I had previously broken myself of the same bad habit. Kaiti tried ignoring, glaring at, sneering at, huffing at, puffing at, and trying to blow off our only parental rule:

Firkins family rule: "In everything you do, do it with respect."

Throughout this challenging year marked by Kaiti's frequent, deliberately disrespectful acts, we tried many creative disciplinary tactics. At every turn, she was chastised, punished, shamed, and otherwise penalized. For example, mouthing off on a summer mini-vacation earned her a whole week of being grounded. (Let me tell you how much fun a vacation can be with a grounded pre-teen and an annoyed mom: no fun at all.) My daughter chose to reply to this measure of discipline with glares and disrespect. So I chose to add an extra chore—washing the windows, inside and out. When she rolled her eyes and let out deep sighs at this sentence, I added trash duty to it. West Texas winds and 15 acres of trash still did not convince her that respectful communication was a better route.

One Sunday afternoon a bit later, my daughter and I were preparing to spend the afternoon at my sister's house for some family fun of scrapbooking and eating. To my amazement, on the holiest of all days (Sabbath yes, but scrapbooking, too) Kaiti popped off with an attitude. In complete frustration—and mainly because the clothes were in my line of sight—I gave her what I considered to be the most horrible of all punishments: the laundry. I picked up a heavy, heaping laundry basket full of mismatched socks, shoved them into her petite frame, and proclaimed, "You will stay home alone and fold these socks, and you will not come down to eat until every last sock has been matched with its perfect counterpart." Before she could utter a response, I left, letting the front door slam behind me, muttering all the way. "How dare this angel of a child think that she can disrespect me or this family?"

Kaiti will tell you that this was the worst punishment of her life. Sitting at home alone, sorting, matching and folding four people's terribly jumbled mess of socks proved to be a turning point in her life.

At last, my consistency as a parent had paid off! The creativity I used in disciplining her burned a hole right through her disrespectful attitude. In its place blossomed one of the most beautiful, assertive—and respectful—children I could have ever imagined.

Interestingly, this was also the point when she made a serious fashion tradition that continues to this day: wearing mismatched socks. Not a day goes by that she doesn't wear two distinctly different socks. It's as if in her silent, respectful way, she is telling me, "Take these socks and stuff 'em!"

SUDSY SUGGESTIONS

Limit the number of mismatched socks in your house by using a safety pin to pair socks together at the toe before washing.

It's a Family Affair . . . Or, Maybe Not?

Train kids (and hubby, too) to fold over their socks at the top before tossing into the hamper.

Just wear one style, one color. Buy all white socks—that way, it doesn't matter if you lose one because they all match.

Buy a mesh laundry bag and clothespin it to the front of each hamper. Have each family member put his or her socks in that little bag. Toss the bag in the washer—no more lost socks!

Kathy Firkins is a Celebrate Moms' Team Member and lives in Texas.

THE BUSINESS OF DOING LAUNDRY

Carla Edmisten

"If I had enough money, I'd pay someone to do laundry for me." I had said that to myself countless times as I opened the dryer door to the next load, which was threatening to force me to iron if I didn't hang up its contents immediately.

Those words came back to me with sudden revelation when my husband and I were discussing the possibility of my starting a home-based business. I could have gone back to the social service field and used my bachelor's degree, but doing that would require day care, and it would rule out field trips with the kids and bagels with my mom friends after drop-off. We did need the extra income, but we were not willing to sacrifice what we considered to be the many advantages of my being a stay-at-home mom.

So after several hours of brainstorming in our living room, my home-based laundry business, "All Washed Up," was born. Start-up costs were minimal, advertising was simple, and best of all, I would be in complete control of my schedule. We thought the plan just might work. And so it did. Within a month, I had signed on enough clients that I was able to make a profit. Word of the new service spread quickly as my customers shared their exhilaration at having their clean laundry delivered to their door. Their linens arrived neatly folded in crisp white bags, and their shirts were starched, ironed to order, and covered in plastic, just like at the cleaners.

Despite the success of my business, I admit I did struggle with the insecurity of being known as the "Laundry Lady." At least in my mind, the term "taking in laundry" had always been associated with the poor and struggling, and I didn't especially like the implication that I had no qualifications that suited me for more "respectable" employment.

Most of my clients were moms who lived in spacious homes with laundry rooms twice as big as mine. Their clothes, along with those of their children, sported high-end labels from stores I never visited. But the stains were all too familiar. Juice from boxes squeezed too tightly by little hands trickled muted pink down the fronts of shirts. And socks showed evidence of trips through the yard taken by little kids who couldn't wait to put on their shoes.

As I drove through elegant subdivisions to pick up or deliver loads, the buzz of mowers and weed cutters offered assurance that the lawn services were maintaining the residents' perfectly manicured lawns.

In contrast, the insides of the homes were silent. Although I had permission to enter through the unlocked doors, I couldn't help but feel as if I were trespassing in museums after hours. Spotlessly clean and adorned in elegance, the homes seemed cavernous compared to our modest home we had long since outgrown. They were spacious and beautiful, all right . . . but they were empty.

Seeing idle toys strewn on the floor of one client's family room stirred up in my mind a slow-motion slide show of my own home: My little man teetering around our kitchen while I emptied the dishwasher . . . his playing "music" on the pots and pans while I fixed lunch . . . the first day he toddled back from the mailbox toward the house by himself when a monarch butterfly flew down to gently kiss the top of his head . . . and the day I found him drinking from the gallon container of apple juice and I had to take pictures before cleaning up the mess.

The strike of an elegant grandfather clock in the client's

foyer abruptly ended my private video. Turning my attention back to the business at hand, I hoisted the bags into the back of my truck and made my way home to my washing machine.

It may not have been the most highly coveted job, I concluded, but I had made it my own, I had made it a success and, more importantly, it was giving me the opportunity to make many more memories with my son.

LAUNDRY'S LIFE LESSON

"Remember this—that there is a proper dignity and proportion to be observed in the performance of every act of life."
—Marcus Aurelius Antoninus

Carla Edmisten lives in Fredericksburg, VA with her husband of 18 years, daughter, Shelby, and son, Logan. Her work has been published in Teatime Stories for Moms, the Chicken Soup Series *and* Southern Arts Journal.

SECTION 7

Oops!

LESSONS FROM A DRYER DOOR

Debbie Salter Goodwin

I heard the sound first—a whop and thud, with reverberating metallic whings. The silence that followed scared me— I feared that Lisa had fallen. She was 12 at the time, and we lived every day afraid of falls because her body was forever limited by juvenile rheumatoid arthritis. A replaced front tooth would always remind us of a childhood fall down four concrete steps.

I headed for the laundry room where I expected to find her in a silent heap on the floor. I was not prepared for what I saw. Lisa stood beside the dryer with her eyes opened wider than her rimmed glasses. At her feet lay the door to the dryer.

"What happened?" I asked, my adrenaline rush still in overdrive.

"The door fell off," she replied.

By this time her father had joined us. We looked at each other and began asking what we thought were obvious questions, "What did you do? How did it happen? How could a door just fall off?"

I quickly realized that our rapid fire questions were paralyzing her, so I returned to my Missouri roots and asked Lisa to "show me" what she had been doing when the door left its hinges. She pantomimed bending over the front-loading dryer door while trying to reach inside. The action she demonstrated meant that she had rested her full weight on the open dryer door. Dryer doors weren't constructed to hold a 90-pound pre-adolescent. Of course it "fell off"!

I wish I could say that I calmly addressed Lisa to show her my understanding that dryer doors were not as important to me as she was. Instead, I let all my fears tumble out

100

Oops!

like wet clothes out of a dryer without a door. "What are we going to do without a dryer door? Do appliance repairmen fix dryer doors? Can we wire it back on?" I could see myself fainting while trying to hold the dryer door in place during a 30-minute timed dry.

That's when my husband, ever the compass when I'm disoriented, offered a simple solution.

"Looks like it's time for a new dryer."

I had been so distressed by the broken door that it never occurred to me that there was a plus side to this disaster. We could get a new dryer!

Now that gave me a good reason to do laundry. Within the week, we had a new dryer—complete with features that actually shortened my laundry time. And Lisa learned not to lean on dryer doors.

But what would she lean on? How could I teach her the importance of checking weight limits before asking a person, or even a dream, to support her? How could I prevent her from devastating falls when someone she depended on let her down?

It would take more than learning not to lean on dryer doors. It would take learning to lean on God. I already knew that Lisa would have to confront major challenges because of a complicated set of mental and physical limitations. She needed to know that God could handle the weight of her grief when a dream died. She needed to know that God could help her carry long-held hopes that shouldn't die. She needed to know that she could throw the whole weight of her anxieties upon him—1 Peter 5:7. Come to think of it, I need the leaning lessons from a dryer door as much as Lisa.

Don't we all?

LOAD LIGHTENERS

A normal 12-pound dryer load goes into the dryer as 20 pounds. It has to lose one gallon of water to dry.

Drying a small load can actually take longer because it reduces the tumbling action. Add a couple of white, dry towels to speed drying.

Drying consecutive loads is energy-efficient because a warmed dryer does the work faster.

You can pour two capfuls of fabric softener onto a towel (used only for this purpose) and use it to dry 12 to 15 loads before adding more softener.

Debbie Salter Goodwin is author of 11 books including The Praying Parent *and* Empowering Your Child Who Has Special Needs. *She lives in Beaverton, Oregon, with her husband Mark.*

Oops!

BLEACH BLUNDERS

Melinda Hines

Not too long ago, I was hastily pouring bleach into the washing machine and splashed some of it on the clothes I was wearing. It forever ruined my beautiful turquoise pants and matching turquoise-and-white-checked shirt. Ugh! I was devastated. The outfit was adorable, and because I had gotten it for a steal at a re-sale shop, it was irreplaceable.

Inadvertently bleaching one of my favorite outfits caused me to ask myself how many times I've splashed my anger and frustration on my family as I have gone throughout my busy day trying to get it all done. Instead of following the admonishments from Scripture such as Proverbs 12:18, "Reckless words pierce like a sword, but the tongue of the wise brings healing," I have, more often than I care to admit, let my irritability and personal problems bleach the color out of my children and my husband.

As moms, we have a profound ability to affect the entire family's mood and behavior. That old saying, "If Momma ain't happy, ain't nobody happy," can be true. While it's difficult to watch what we say, it's critical that we remember the impact of our words is long lasting, if not permanent. I can still remember negative words from my own childhood that colored who I am as a woman, wife, and mom today. Just like those turquoise pants and matching checked shirt, my heart has splotchy marks from where hurtful words washed over me, lifting the color off the fabric of my spirit.

I tried unsuccessfully to bleach the outfit completely and evenly in order to dye it another color, bringing to mind times when I've tried to use positive thoughts to bring balance to words my loved ones have said to me in anger and pain. But sometimes, like the turquoise outfit, the damage is beyond repair.

Abraham Lincoln once said, "It takes nine affirming comments to make up for each critical comment we give to our children." Let me encourage you to say something kind to your children today and to keep your critical comments to yourself. Allow your love for them to seep into the bleached spots of their hearts, creating a lasting feeling that can't be ruined.

SUDSY SUGGESTIONS

Unless the garment label specifically says it is okay, don't use bleach. Use bleach only on white and colorfast washables, and always read fabric care labels first.

Never use chlorine bleach on silk, wool, spandex, nylon, or fabrics with flame-resistant finishes.

Use fabric/oxygen bleach, which comes in dry and liquid forms, with most washable silks and woolens as long as they are colorfast.

Avoid creating bleach splotches and even small holes in the garments by adding chlorine bleach to the water before you add the clothes. Use the bleach dispenser, if your machine has one.

Be careful using chlorine bleach if your household water supply has a high iron content; it can draw out the iron and deposit it as small rust stains.

Never mix chlorine bleach with any other cleaning agent; it can create toxic fumes.

Melinda Hines is a Celebrate Moms' Team Member and lives in Texas.

Oops!

PINK

Melissa Evans

Pink. Not a popular color in my testosterone-filled household. Pink t-shirts, socks, and underwear are fine for me . . . but not for my husband and two sons. I try to tell them that many stylish—and very manly—men wear pink, but they just don't buy it. They prefer to stick to their blacks, blues, greys and whites. How, then, was I going to explain this to them?

I am usually very conscientious when I do the laundry. With two young sons, I've become an expert at pre-treating stains—did you know that human spit can get out blood-stains?—and at double checking pockets for things like rocks, crayons, trading cards, and the occasional critter. Then how did this load of whites turn out to be such a pretty shade of . . . you guessed it . . . pink?

As I dug through the load—trying to decide how I was going to convince my men that pink was the new black—I discovered the problem. Somehow, a single red sock had hitch-hiked its way into my load of whites. That one unnoticed, unchecked sock had infiltrated the purity of the inner sanctum of my machine and polluted everything it came into contact with. All the while, I was completely unaware that a problem existed—until it was too late.

At first, I thought that perhaps no one would notice. I mean, it's not like my guys had ever paid a great deal of attention to laundry before. However, one glance at my youngest son's favorite soccer shirt dashed any hopes of that. He might not pay much attention to laundry, but he would definitely know that soccer balls were black and white . . . not black and pink. How was I going to remedy this situation—short of going out and buying all new socks, underwear and shirts for three-quarters of my family?

Fortunately, that answer came in a little square box marked RIT Color Remover. Until this incident, I didn't even know that such a product existed, and I certainly didn't have much hope in it actually working. However, desperate times call for desperate measures, and at this point I was edging up to desperate so I purchased the box, read the instructions, and gave it a shot. To my relief and amazement, it worked like a charm. The threat to my men's masculinity had abated. Their whites were gloriously restored to white.

Though my husband and boys knew nothing about their close call with feminine fashion, the whole incident got me thinking: If only every mess in life came with a little square box of miracle powder that could remove the "pink." That's when it occurred to me that I don't need a lifetime supply of RIT (though admittedly that might come in handy); instead, I have access to the greatest stain remover to ever exist—Jesus.

I recalled a verse from Scripture that I had memorized as a child: Isaiah 1:18 says that "Though your sins are like scarlet, they shall be as white as snow . . . ." I'm no theologian, but even as a child I knew those words were not referring to laundry. They were referring to sin.

You see, we may think that things are going just fine in our lives. Okay, sure, we tell a white lie here and there, or we fudge a little on our job, but those are only small things; it's not like we're out robbing banks or stealing cars after all. What we don't realize however; is that those little indiscretions are just like that one red sock. Though we might not think that our little "slips" are doing any real damage, the truth is that they are secretly coloring all our thoughts and behaviors—often without us even realizing that we are gradually being changed from pure white to shades of scarlet.

Oops!

Eventually, we discover that a problem exists—but it is usually only after the damage has been done, and we are faced with a mess of our own making.

That's why I am so thankful for the saving grace Jesus offers. No matter how pink (or scarlet) we've become, Jesus can clean up the mess and restore us back to purity. My pink laundry episode definitely taught me a lesson about diligence. I now keep better watch out for red socks in my whites and for "little" sins in my life, but it also taught me about redemption.

SUDSY SUGGESTION

Hard water can often cause clothes to become dull or dingy after a few washings. To solve this problem, try adding a couple of pinches of ordinary table salt to the washer with the detergent. You'll want to let some water run in the washer to dissolve the detergent and salt before you add your clothes, but you'll be amazed at how this little trick will brighten up your dingy colors.

Melissa Evans lives at the base of the Rocky Mountains in Loveland, Colorado, with her husband Randy and two young sons.

TEA-STAINED LAUNDRY

Sandy McKeown

Mountainous piles of dirty laundry. How had it gotten so bad? I dug in and sorted, washed, dried, and folded the countless piles of clothes a family of six creates. It was well past midnight and everyone else was in bed when I finished. I didn't want to disturb my sleeping cherubs while putting their clothes away, so I piled the neatly folded laundry back into baskets and left them in a tidy row on the laundry room floor, planning to complete my marathon in the morning after everyone was up. After one last satisfied look at all I had accomplished, I went upstairs to get some needed rest.

"Daddy, I need you," whispered our five-year-old while trying to nudge my husband awake. I squinted up from my side of the bed; my son was hunched over his dad, obviously trying not to disturb me. Whatever was going on just after sun's early light, he didn't want me to know about it. I went back to sleep, confident my husband could handle whatever minor calamity was happening downstairs.

Later, when I ventured down, I discovered the kitchen floor had been freshly mopped. Hands on hips, I asked suspiciously, "What happened?"

My husband reluctantly informed me that our early riser had decided to help himself to a bowl of cereal—nothing unusual about that—but when he reached into the refrigerator to retrieve the milk, a very large pitcher of iced tea was blocking it. He tried lifting the pitcher out of the way, but spilled the entire contents all over the floor instead.

I shrugged, "No harm done." But that wasn't the end of the story. My husband informed me our usually single-minded child hadn't known what to do, so while the tea pooled in a brown puddle on our oak floor, he went into the living room and sat on the couch to ponder his choices.

Oops!

I'm not sure what thoughts went through his mind, but I do wish they had developed faster. Because while he was thinking in the living room, the tea was seeping through the slats of the oak floor in the kitchen and dripping down into the laundry room on all my freshly washed laundry.

Not only did I have to re-wash the majority of the clothes, but several of the stains wouldn't come out, including those on a shirt my husband had worn only once. Stubborn tea stains forced me to toss out several favorite clothes.

Of course, I didn't feel I could scold or discipline my innocent angel, but I did have a few words with my husband for blocking the milk with the tea pitcher. What was he thinking? Hadn't we discussed proactive parenting and consistently meeting the needs of our children to avoid problems? I wasn't exactly crying over spilled iced tea, but I was pointing out obvious ways this problem could have been avoided. Wasn't that helpful of me?

The cycle of our third son creating havoc, Dad quietly cleaning it up, and Mom finding out about it later became a long-lasting pattern for us—one that usually ended in a marital spat. It may be no surprise that several years later we ended up in counseling—the three of us—for two years during this child's teenage days. How had the conflicts, the miscommunication, and everyday life gotten so bad?

Just as our son ignored the spilled tea while mulling over his choices that day, resulting in bigger problems, our family ignored the communication problems that were seeping through our lives.

As adults, we often brood over our options—too often and too long—which only exacerbates the problem. It was a long time before the stains of resentment, anger, and unforgiveness intensified until my family could no longer ignore them. But unlike the stained laundry that I had ultimately discarded, we couldn't give up on each other. These stains needed professional treatment, and we had to face the problems we could not remove ourselves.

Does your family have stains you can't get out? Don't give up on them; get some professional help to get them out.

LAUNDRY'S LIFE LESSON
"When you've tried, and you are unable to fix it yourself, get help." —Tom Jacobs, Sioux City, Iowa

Sandy McKeown is a Celebrate Moms' Team Member and lives in Iowa.

Oops!

SNOW TIDE

Gail Cawley Showalter

When Lance, my third child, was born, I had a three-year-old girl, Treva, and an 18-month-old boy, Damon. That's three kids in 37 months—an exhausting season of my life.

When Lance was about two, I made the mistake of putting my feet up for a nanosecond when Treva, the quintessential big sister, came to me.

"Mommy, I think you better come see what the boys have done."

I thought, "What could a two- and four-year-old do in a few seconds?"

At the far end of the bedroom hallway was a custom laundry room. On a bright day, the sunlight streamed in through the windows above the washer, dryer, and sink. There was a built-in sewing machine and large laundry bins. This room was exceptionally cheery and in frequent use. I bought detergent in the largest boxes available—they were about the size of small microwaves.

On this particular day as Treva led me down the hall, I got a chill. A frost was drifting in from the far end of the hallway. I shivered and then saw a powdery cloud billowing through the laundry room door. There was a snowstorm, or better said, a blizzard in the house!

"It's snowing!" I heard a tiny snow bunny exclaim, followed by a squeal of delight. Then came more laughter and more squeals.

I surveyed the glistening vision of white that covered every surface, even the eye of the needle in my sewing machine. Finger-painting swirls made with soapy fingers frosted the windows. Tiny hands and large imaginations had

111

flung every grain of detergent that drifted like a snowflake to the surface below.

It might have been the calm after the storm, had it not been for the geyser that was spewing from the sink faucet. Damon had decided he would repair a leak and removed the faucet head. As the water sprayed over the new-fallen snow, a sludge of suds was swiftly forming.

There was no point in screaming. This was a childhood experience born out of curiosity and imagination—both traits I tried to encourage.

After turning off the water source, I grabbed Lance firmly and sat him on his beloved bum. He slid across the floor as the surface oozed underneath him.

"Stay there," I said, knowing nothing could stay in place on this slime.

Turning to Damon, I ordered, "Bring me a broom." I was optimistic to think a broom would work on suds.

In his childish innocence, he bargained, "If I do, will I get a treat?" He thought he would take advantage of the re-ward-for-obedience program I had implemented. His request almost pushed me over the edge. But in that moment, I passed the ultimate mothering test: I did not clobber my son. I simply tackled the task at hand.

The broom failed, and then I tried the vacuum, but soon heard a whirling and whining. Looking down into the metal tube, I saw a gooey coating of soapy emulsion clinging to the inside of my vacuum cleaner. Cleaning up soap is a messy job.

When we sold the house a few years later, it seemed to me that the buyers gave a little shiver and hugged themselves when they entered the snow room. They looked puzzled, but I knew the reason. With their imaginations and a big box of detergent, my little snow bunnies had forever

Oops!

turned the place into a magical winter wonderland. The snowstorm in the laundry room remains a fond family memory. Perhaps that's because I didn't allow my temper to turn it into a national disaster.

> ### LAUNDRY'S LIFE LESSON
> "Adults teach children in three important ways: The first is by example; the second is by example; the third is by example." —Albert Schweitzer

Gail Showalter was a single mother of three for 16 years. Now that she is remarried and her children are grown, she writes, speaks, and is building a ministry for single moms.

PINEAPPLE UNDERWEAR

Kara Lee Mantinaos

When my normally sweet and compliant 10-year-old son recently grumbled about his afternoon obligation to put away the clean laundry, I couldn't get annoyed or frustrated because I used to complain about it, too. My complaining, however, came in the form of procrastination and was evidence of my own bad attitude and lax habits. I have always been great at getting the laundry started; it's in the follow-through that I fall down. This is true for many of my undertakings. But as a replacement for the self-assault that used to follow my habitual procrastination, I've developed strategies to gently remind myself to "get with the program," "just do it," and above all else, "get my heart right." At our house, this is known as the "Pineapple Underwear Principle."

To understand this, you will need a little background information. My handsome husband does not like the pineapple-print underwear I purchased for him. He will wear them, but only as a last resort, insisting they are not as comfortable as his other pairs in nice, solid colors. But I think it's because, in his sartorially conservative mind, he finds pineapples too whimsical for "unmentionables" belonging to a man of his stature. Either way, I certainly don't want him to be uncomfortable physically or mentally, so I keep the pineapple pairs as spares, tucked neatly at the bottom of the stack.

The two pairs have come to serve as mellow reminders that, when they're in use, it's time for me to get back to the structure and discipline of the effective routines that keep our household happy.

When my husband used to ask, "Did you do the laundry?" it always felt to me like an accusation. But his casual mention that he's donned a pair of pineapple boxers tenderly lets me know that he is dangerously low on undies and this particular area of our household routine needs attention. It's a red flag, if you will, disguised as pineapple underwear.

Routines and structure are not part of my essential makeup, you see. Being creative and imaginative can translate into being ineffective and scatterbrained when faced with many small, but important, tasks on a daily basis. In hopes of thwarting these detrimental patterns in the lives of my progeny, I'm trying to teach them routines so they can run their lives with greater efficiency than I have previously run mine. More importantly, I don't want them wasting their gifts on habit-breaking or the frustration that comes with a cluttered environment, mind, or life.

If you, too, are creative or free-spirited, routines may sound restrictive or oppressive as they did to me at first. Yet they have given us a wonderful freedom because our household and our relationships run more smoothly when both our space and our hearts are clutter-free.

Our hearts? Yes. Let me give you an example. When we run late in the morning and my son and I get frustrated with each other, we can talk about it later in a non-threatening manner when I say, "What was the Pineapple Underwear this morning?" Without having to nag—I'm saying, "If you had prepared your notebook (or music or gym clothes) the previous night, we wouldn't have encountered negativity this morning." When I am snippy or, shamefully downright ugly toward one of my family members, they throw the Pineapple Underwear my way, saying with patience and longsuffering, "The way you're acting isn't loving or positive. Please get your heart right."

And when that normally sweet 10-year-old throws his

dad's actual Pineapple Underwear down the steps, he is earnestly, yet humorously, telling us to please get his little sister away from him and give him some space so he can just be 10 years old and go grumble and complain in solitude. He then goes to tinker around in his room and talk to God until his heart is right. Afterward, when he rejoins the family fellowship, it is intact, thanks to the Pineapple Underwear.

LAUNDRY'S LIFE LESSON
For wonderful help with establishing effective laundry and other routines—like menu planning, exercise, and weight loss—please introduce yourself to FLYLady at www.flylady.net. She'll teach you how to get the laundry done (and put away!), how to get your heart right, and how to F-L-Y: Finally Love Yourself.

Kara Lee Mantinaos lives in western Pennsylvania with her young family. Some of her works include Does God Care What I Wear? *and* Baby in the Breadbasket: Our Miracle Adoption from Ukraine.

SECTION 8

Without Spot Or Wrinkle

IN THE NICK OF TIME

Cassandra Woods

"Hey guys, come on. We've got to get going." That's standard jargon in my household, on school mornings at least. Things usually go pretty smoothly, unless we had waited until that morning to choose the day's outfit. If you're one of those mothers who plans out the family's clothes for the week, bear with me, please. I'm sure I risk my family falling over their shoes in disbelief when I say this, but I am not the "perfect" mom. Gasp. I can sense their shock as I write.

On one of those not-so-smooth mornings, my son decided he didn't want to wear the previously chosen outfit. After all, looking neat, wearing a shirt that's really your size, and a belt to keep your pants around your waist is considered "lame." So he decided he was going to wear his coveted nylon Michael Vick jersey.

I can say this, he was concerned enough about his looks to know that the jersey needed to be wrinkle-free. Unknown to me, he headed for the laundry room. As I entered the kitchen, I heard sounds of movement coming from that direction.

Upon further investigation, I discovered him with the red and black #7 (iron-on) jersey spread across the ironing board and the hot iron in hand. I looked at the jersey. I looked at him. My mind quickly registered what the end result would be, so in a calm but stern authoritative voice, I said, "Stop!" Okay maybe it wasn't all that calm, and yes it may have sounded more like a shriek, but it got the job done. After getting his attention, I proceeded, "Put the iron down."

"But I want to wear it," he said.

Realizing he was still holding the steaming iron. I re-

118

sorted to a more mellow tone. "But you'll mess it up like that," I said. "You'll burn a hole right through it."

I could see the decision to surrender in his eyes. At that moment he set the iron down and moved away from the ironing board. The unsuspecting jersey was saved, just in the nick of time.

Sometimes I wonder how many times my children have been saved from other detrimental acts. Whether on the ball field or track, whether toddling or driving, God always seems to protect them. He gives them a thought. Maybe they remember something I said or did—an encouraging word, a hug, or a smile. When they find themselves in a bad situation, something makes them stop in their tracks and make a better choice.

What a responsibility for a mother! Just to think that one word I say to my children at one moment in time could change the course of their destiny. And I never know when that moment will occur.

What if it comes when I have run myself so ragged that I'm too tired to interact with them? What if the moment comes, and I am allowing myself to harbor unforgiveness and am short with them? What if the moment comes and I am not sure of my own self worth—what can I say to them then? For me the risk is too great to take. I must do what I can to take care of myself so I will have strength in spirit, mind, and body to pass along the right words to those in my care—words that will build up and not tear down, words that will be a blessing and not a curse. I must be committed to nurture them. I must find the patience to wait for them to mature. I must love them from my overflow.

There is a time to speak and a time to remain quiet. There is a time to correct and a time to have mercy. Don't be afraid. You'll know. Listen to that still, small voice. That may be the moment you or your child will be saved—just in the nick of time.

LOAD LIGHTENERS

It is okay to do something just for you. Say it right now. "I give myself permission to do something that I enjoy." Mothers are used to sacrificing their wants and desires for their family. However, it is important to you and your children that you continue to nurture yourself. Whether it is a few minutes or a few days, find time to do something you love....

Read a novel.
Have lunch with a friend.
Take a bubble bath.
Visit a site in your city that you've never gone to before.
Buy yourself a greeting card.

It's easy to do something nice for others, so why not do something nice for you? Start today.

Cassandra Woods is a Celebrate Moms' Team Member and lives in Alabama.

STAIN QUEEN

Melinda Hines

My husband calls me his stain queen, not only because I seem to stain things often, but because I have made it my personal mission to remove the stains from our lives. I abhor seeing an item ruined and then spending money to replace it.

Sometimes a quality pre-treatment spray or stain stick may be all it takes to remove stains. However, sometimes we have to pull out all the stops and ask a professional for help, like the time our daughter accidentally marked on our brand-new comforter with a green marker. She pointed out the ominous streaks of green during a tear-filled confession, and fortunately I was able to get most of it off with a baby wipe, followed by a stain pre-treater. Soon after, I noticed pen marks on the same comforter. I lifted those off easily with a thorough dousing of good, old-fashioned aerosol hairspray. When my daughter later threw up on the same comforter, it took repeated washings and a few expensive trips to the cleaners to restore the bedding to its original color and fresh smell.

Caring for my children can require a similar strategy. At times, a simple hug, a kind word, or a gentle reminder is all it takes to soothe and assure them that I love them and that everything will be all right. But sometimes, I have to increase my efforts—and, at times, even ask a professional for help—in order to teach them these things.

When your child has a broken heart stained with pain and disappointment, it may take chocolates and a box of tissues to mend it. When he or she is ill or struggling in school, you may need to seek help from doctors or counselors.

Even though I eventually gave up on getting the myriad

of stains out of that comforter and bought another one, I am thankful to know God doesn't give up on us or our children.

SUDSY SUGGESTIONS
Stain Removal 101

Keep a portable stain kit filled with cleansers and towels handy in the car and at home because speed is the key to successfully removing stains.

Products such as Shout wipes, Tide pens, and even baby wipes will take care of most fresh stains.

It is essential to treat stains before you do the laundry. That's because stains are set by heat; once a stain has been washed in warm water and heat-dried, it is difficult, if not impossible, to remove.

Always test stain removal products on an inconspicuous spot of the clothing.

Blot, never rub, a fresh stain.

Prevent the stain from spreading by working the cleaning agent from the edges of the spot to its center.

Apply the cleaning agent to the underside of the fabric to force the stain out.

Be patient and persistent; you may need to repeat a treatment a few times to see results. When in doubt, dry clean.

Melinda Hines is a Celebrate Moms' Team Member and lives in Texas.

SEEING RED

Anna Marie Warren

I have a jar in the laundry room that holds all the treasures that I discover as I dig through the clothes on laundry day. Most of the time, my finds consist of small coins, rocks, jewelry, lip-gloss, or paper money. Because the rule in our house is, "If Mom finds it she keeps it," most weeks I find enough valuables to support my Sunday-on-the-way-to-church Starbucks habit.

Out of the entire family, my husband is the best about checking his pockets to make sure they're empty before he puts his dirty clothes in the laundry basket. He is so good, in fact, that I don't even check his pockets anymore.

However, one particular day I was doing a load of his dress shirts—which I handle carefully because he is so neat and I am not—when I heard the familiar buzz call me to the laundry room, signaling that it was time to take his shirts out of the dryer.

I opened the dryer door to find a jumble of shirts I had never seen before. Each one sported a distinct pattern of "tumble-me red." After I recovered from my panic attack, I unearthed a red pen that had been a stowaway in one of my husband's shirt pockets and had received the daily wash-n-dry special.

I was horrified. What should I do? (Did I mention this load included all of my husband's dress shirts?)

My first thought was to run to the store and buy all new shirts to replace the ones that were ruined and hope he would never know the difference. But reality instantly took hold of me. First, I didn't have that much time before he came home; second, a shopping spree wasn't in our budget (plus, shopping isn't nearly as much fun when you aren't shopping for yourself); and third, I could never pull off a charade like that because even though I'm very resourceful and confident in my ability to overcome obstacles, I was dealing with a man who notices when something is out of place within five seconds after he walks into a room. You know the type.

So I had to come up with a different plan and decided to start with the basics: stain remover. Only there wasn't a bottle of it in the house. I dug through every cabinet, every drawer—nothing.

Think, think, think. I just needed some kind of spray. I had to act fast because he would be home any minute. I got it! I had a 99¢ can of hairspray, which I promptly emptied onto the shirts and began scrubbing in. Then, I threw the colorful load into the washer for another ride in the machine. I didn't even look at the clothes before I transferred them to the dryer. I didn't really want to know.

As my husband arrived home, the dryer buzzed again. Being the helper that he is, my husband joined me in the laundry room to hang and button the shirts. I was relieved to discover that the hairspray had removed all traces of the ink—all traces, that is, except for a small red mark on one of the shirt pockets.

Who do you think noticed it first?

LAUNDRY'S LIFE LESSON

Since my red pen episode, I have used hairspray many times to remove stains. Spray and pump varieties work equally well. Saturate the stained area, rub, and wash immediately.

SUDSY SUGGESTION

When the dryer buzzer cries out to you, you had better hurry and hang up the clothes before they wrinkle, or else you will be stuck ironing all day—or drying the same load over and over. In cases of emergency, just buy the spray that takes away all the wrinkles without an iron.

Anna Marie Warren is a Celebrate Moms' Team Member and lives in Texas.

SOILED LINENS

Tonya Holter

The big day was here! Our third and youngest child would become officially potty trained. I had successfully potty trained in a day my first two children by following a technique I found in a book, so I was certain that I had already mastered the fine art. This time, I figured, would be a breeze.

I greeted the day with much enthusiasm and optimism, and wasn't disappointed: My two-year-old son did a great job of staying dry all day long. At bedtime, I tucked him in with a passionate potty-training pep talk, setting the stage exactly as I had done with my other two children. "This is it," I thought as I rolled into my own bed. "Our first dry night!"

But the next morning, my heart sank as I discovered my sweet potty-trainee was wet from head to toe. I was shocked! My failproof plan wasn't supposed to work this way! Our other two kids had learned this technique very quickly. What had gone wrong?

As I eventually found out, that wasn't to be the day our youngest would become potty trained after all. Rather, it was to be the first day of our long journey down a trying path called bed-wetting. I wasn't too discouraged at first, but after our little one continued to have accidents night after night, year after year, I had finally accepted the fact that I had a bed-wetter.

At first, we had our son wear disposable training pants every night. That made middle-of-the-night slip-ups easy to handle . . . until he began to notice that he was wearing a "diaper," as he called it. From then on, he refused to wear the uncomfortable disposable pants, ushering us into a whole new routine. Laundering wet bed linens was now a daily chore.

Without Spot Or Wrinkle

Washing those soaked bed sheets and damp comforters along with soggy pajamas and underwear every day for the past ten years has given me a unique set of laundry-related challenges. There's daily frustration over the added work it piles onto our already mountainous heap of household laundry. And there's the stress of always having to get those sheets in the wash before I leave the house.

But the biggest challenge of raising a child who wets the bed doesn't have anything to do with the laundry, and it has everything to do with his feelings: Oh, how I have ached for my child! He is the one who really suffers with the embarrassment of midnight accidents, and with the inconvenience of having to make sudden runs to the bathroom to strip off his wet pajamas and take a shower.

Of course, as his mother, I love my son unconditionally—whether or not he wakes up dry each morning. But I think I love him even more when he comes to me with his soiled linens and asks, "Mommy, can you make these clean again?"

In the same moment that I answer, "Of course I will," I am reminded that we, too, can bring our "soiled linens" to God. When we do that, we receive not only His love, but we also receive His cleansing. Through my son and his soiled linens, God has taught me to love in a way that has no strings attached—soiled linens and all.

I believe our big day will come. At some point, our son will be able to stay dry all night. But in the meantime, I will continue to wash his soiled linens every morning, just as our Lord washes us clean and makes us new every morning if we just ask. God loves us unconditionally, but He loves to hear us ask, "Father, can you make me clean again?" And when we are quiet enough, we can hear His still, small voice say, "Yes child, of course I will."

LAUNDRY'S LIFE LESSONS

Approximately 7 million children in the United States suffer from "nocturnal enuresis," or "bed-wetting." The American Psychiatric Association has defined a bed-wetter as a child older than age five who is incontinent of urine at night. If you have a bed-wetter in your family, here are some tips that might help:

Don't scold. Bed-wetting is embarrassing to a child without being reprimanded.
Don't tease or let siblings tease. Teasing can really harm a child's self-esteem.
Don't neglect the problem. Team up with your health care provider to discuss your treatment options.

Do have a positive attitude. This can make all the difference for your child and his or her self-esteem.
Do keep a simple routine. The easier it is to manage the late-night accidents, the better it will be for everyone.
Do your best not to make it a big deal. This will help maintain your child's confidence.

SUDSY SUGGESTIONS

1. Cover mattresses with a plastic waterproof mattress pads.
2. Keep disposable, antibacterial wipes handy for quick and easy clean-up.
3. Buy washable linens only—avoid bulky or dry-clean only linens.
4. Keep an extra set of pillows, sheets and blankets nearby for middle-of-the-night changes.

Tonya Holter is a Celebrate Moms' Team Member and lives in Arkansas.

TABLECLOTHS DON'T COVER EVERYTHING

Dianne Daniels

The sound told me exactly what was happening. As my husband slid the top of my dining room table out of the back of the moving van, I could hear gouges forming. I hurried inside my new home to find something to unpack, deciding I'd examine the damage later—in privacy.

Once the table was nestled into its new dining room, I surveyed the damage. Sure enough, there were two deep, parallel lines exposing light, raw wood against the backdrop of walnut stain. The classic French design now sported pin stripes. I felt panic rising in my throat as I realized that not only was the table damaged, but this was something I wouldn't be able to hide from my relatives. The family table passed down from Grandma had been ruined while it was in my care.

I tried decorating the tabletop with placemats, a centerpiece and decorative foliage like you find in model homes, but eventually accepted the fact that I am no designer. Finally, I confessed to my mother. She told me just to throw a tablecloth over it. I cringed at her words, hoping she'd have a second idea.

"That means I'll have to iron a tablecloth, and I hate ironing. I'm no good at it," I protested.

"Oh no," she assured me. "Just pull it out of the dryer as soon as it's done and take it straight to the table. It will work out fine."

I doubted that. The dryer method of removing wrinkles worked all right for blue jeans, but I had never been able to make a tablecloth look good and had given up trying years before.

But in desperation, I decided to try my mother's suggestion. Because friends and family had given me tablecloths as presents nearly every Christmas (apparently, they thought I didn't own one because they'd never seen one in use in my home), I had somewhere in the neighborhood of nine unused, un-ironed, unfriendly tablecloths. I got them all out and found the one that best fit the table, realizing I'd never be able to invite more than six people to dinner ever again. That would require adding an extension leaf to the table, forcing me to dig out a larger tablecloth.

I ran the cloth through a dust-removing spin in the washing machine and then transferred it to the almighty dryer. When the fluff cycle ended, I whisked the warm tablecloth from the drum, ran to the dining room and flung the material over the table. I wanted it to look like one of those fabric softener commercials where soft, beautiful yards of cotton and silk flow gracefully through the breeze. In reality, the tablecloth did not look lovely, billowy, or even wrinkle-free! I stared at the table in disgust, realizing that while the cloth no longer held deep creases, it still revealed to the world that I don't iron. Now I had to decide which looked worse—the scars in the table or the grid of wrinkles in the cloth.

I don't know why I thought covering the table might work. Hiding has never worked for me, in any area of life. I've tried masking hurt feelings under a smile, disappointment under enthusiasm, and fear under hard work. And while the cover-ups sometimes seem effective for a while, they never hide the truth for long.

What worked best for my broken table turned out to be a trip to a carpenter for refinishing. And what works best for my broken heart is a visit to God for healing. God doesn't hide, and neither will I. He makes the truth clear and easy to find for all who look for it, and that's how I want to be. No more covers.

Without Spot Or Wrinkle

LOAD LIGHTENER

It is no surprise that in the 17th century, people used sadirons or sad irons to smooth their clothes. These devices were triangular slabs of cast iron heated in a fire. While I'm glad we don't use that system today, the name still applies!

Dianne Daniels avoids ironing by spending her days with her husband and two young children at their home in Colorado.

ACIDIC LAUNDRY

Teri Heether

If you do not have the pleasure of raising sons, there is a high probability that you won't relate to what I am about to share. You may not be able to understand the gag reflex caused by male post-game uniforms.

From the camaraderie and the practices to every part of the games, my two young sons loved their sports. They loved them so much, in fact, that they weren't fazed by sweating in the heat, freezing in the winter, or suffering physical pain while striving for victory—accounting for the blood stains on their uniforms. As their mom, I cherished their passionate, single-minded tenacity on the playing field, and I shared in the happiness that sports brought them. To me, the real stars of the game were the players whose laundry I took care of at the end of each event. I may have spent countless hours on the bleachers cheering them on, but I am sure I spent an equal number of hours in solitude attempting to return their uniforms to a level of public acceptability.

As the years went on, I became quite skilled at doing their laundry. With administrative determination, I sprayed scum remover on stained helmets, bleached their sweat-soaked socks, and mended their torn uniforms. I developed strategies for preserving the bright colors, and I learned to soak the garments in baking soda to dissipate the smell.

Football season always ushered in my greatest laundry challenges. Nothing is as shockingly odoriferous as post-football game helmets, pads and jerseys. Apparently, pre-puberty/high-school teenage hormones plus adrenaline and sweat equals a near-toxic stench that only a boy's mom—or someone without olfactory glands—can tolerate. It is a uniquely permanent smell. Once you have whiffed it into your memory tank, it can never be erased.

My job as the boys' "laundry assistant" consumed my schedule for many years. During that time, I prayed I would not begrudge this monotonous chore. Taking care of their uniforms was my way of contributing to their passions and their sports dreams. The Bible says in Philippians 2:14 that we should do all things without complaining. It was a privilege to minister to my sons in this seemingly small way. Often, I would use the moments I spent at the washing machine to pray for them. That was my way of taking a small but vital part in my growing boys' lives as God was doing His job of transforming them into men.

My sons are, in fact, grown now. Not surprisingly, one's a golf pro and the other is a professional baseball player. I am, of course, no longer in charge of doing their laundry. But recently, I walked into a high school gym and instantly recognized the aroma of boys practicing basketball. While my girlfriends who were with me groaned, rolled their eyes, and held their noses, I calmly inhaled, remembering fondly those days of motherhood when those offensive scents punctuated my days.

SUDSY SUGGESTIONS

Football equipment needs to be expunged from its acidic, non-human smell. Immediately after the game, spray antiseptic all over the pads and helmets, particularly focusing on the inside of the helmet. Put the equipment outside in the fresh air until the next practice. Adding baking soda to a load of sports uniforms will help break up the sour smell of the clothes.

Teri Heether and her husband Ricky have two adult sons, Adam and Aaron, and one daughter-in-love, Jennifer. Teri is active in women's ministry leadership.

AVOIDING RUB OFF

Jill Hart

I cringed as I pulled my husband's brand-new shirt from the washing machine. What had I done? Reaching inside the appliance, I searched for—and found—the culprit. Why had I added my husband's shirt to the same load that included our preschool daughter's glitter-covered dance costume? Now my husband's favorite button-down was caked with silver glitter, and it sparkled iridescently at me under the florescent light of the mudroom. Ugh!

Have you ever had something like that happen to you? In your hurry to get the laundry done, you pop something into a load that rubs off onto another piece of clothing? Sometimes the rub-off can be fixed. In this case, I was able to rewash my husband's shirt alone to remove the glitter. However, there have been a few times it wasn't that easy. When, for example, something red ends up washing with the whites, there's no going back. Rub-offs can be disastrous; that's why it's important to take precautions to avoid them.

It may sound strange, but rub-offs can happen in family life, too. When we interact with one another, our attitudes "rub off" on those around us. Many days, I've gotten up "on the wrong side of the bed." Days like these generally begin with my six-month-old baby crying in the wee hours of the morning, long before I'm ready to get up. I stumble into the nursery, pick up Isaac, make my way to the living room, and try to catnap on the couch, grumbling under my breath all the way.

It's not long before our four-year-old Katy bounces out of bed, talking a mile a minute, much like a farm yard rooster announcing the start of an exciting day. She's ready for breakfast and is anticipating her fun day. Meanwhile, my sweet husband remains in bed, sleeping soundly, oblivious to the early morning start with our precious early risers.

By the time I plop a bowl of cereal on the kitchen table, my daughter is aware that this will be "one of those days." Many times she's already grumpy—complaining that she didn't get enough milk or begging me to make muffins for breakfast. Often I'll hear my attitude coming across loudly and clearly in her voice, and I'll catch myself; however, on some days I'm just too exhausted to talk myself into a good humor, and my bad attitude glares starkly in the dim of the morning light.

As moms, our moods and behavior generally set the tone for the entire household. I've had days when I've seen my bad attitude rub off on everyone in my family—even the dog!

It's easy to put a stop to laundry rub-off: Just sort those clothes carefully! But how do we combat the attitude rub-off? Here are some tips:

First, we can take a deep breath and remind ourselves that in the big scheme of things, we have it pretty good. We have a roof over our heads, children we love and who love us back most of the time. If the weather is fair, it helps to step outside and breathe in the fresh air. The beauty surrounding us can help us remember that each day is a gift.

Second, we can give our kids a big hug. They probably won't be expecting it, and they may even resist it if our attitude has rubbed off on them! But it's surprising how much power one little hug has in dissolving the stubborn stain of bad attitude rub-off. If we give each child some physical affection and a kind word, we'll be well on our way to a "good attitude" kind of day.

Third, we can make a list of things that we are grateful for. This may seem silly, but I did this when I was a newlywed, and it really helped. Once I realized that I was sporting a particularly bad attitude and began to see its effects on my husband, I realized I needed to make a change. So I started an inventory of all the things I appreciated about him. I do the same thing now for my children, jotting down things I simply love about each of them. On days when my attitude needs a boost, I review my list. Inevitably, every item I read makes me smile. And who can have a bad attitude when she has a great big grin on her face? There's no better reminder of how wonderful our families are than to see their good qualities written in our own handwriting. (Be sure to hang your list someplace prominent, perhaps in the mudroom under the fluorescent lights with a little glitter sprinkled across the paper!)

LOAD LIGHTENER

Wash your children's clothing in a separate load from your own. You just never know what may be in those little pockets.

Jill Hart is a Celebrate Moms' Team Member and lives in Nebraska.

SECTION 9

Gotta Love 'Em!

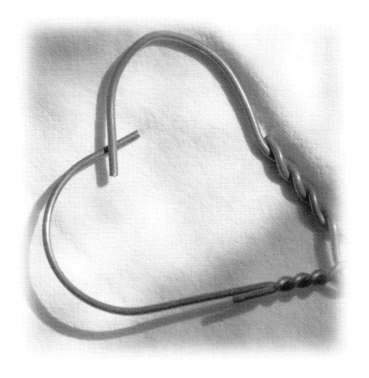

AIRING YOUR DIRTY LAUNDRY

Jami Kirkbride

Ching, bonk, ching, bonk. The sound beckoned me from the far side of the house. Exasperated, I shuffled to the laundry room and opened the door of the washing machine to discover what might be making the unusual banging this time. I unloaded each item of clothing and wondered what would be at the bottom of the pile. My tension increased as I wondered about the value of the object I was likely to find. Then I spotted it—a gold watch. It had not weathered the wash very well. It was shining, but it wasn't ticking.

It only took one guess to figure out how it had gotten there. We had a three-year-old son who was full of curiosity. While we worked tirelessly to tame his precocious nature, we were far more concerned with the safety of his pursuits. I found him playing and explained once again that the washing machine was only for clothes.

"Just clothes," I emphasized again.

"But how does Daddy wash his watch?" He asked with a serious look on his face.

"I don't know, but not in the washing machine!" I said with frustration.

Bammm! Bammm! Bammm! I had been putting on my makeup when I heard a frightening, thunderous noise. I immediately dropped my mascara and ran through the house. As I neared the laundry room, I could tell the noise was coming from there. But this was not the sound of something banging in the dryer, it was far worse.

Scared half to death, I peeked around the corner. There I saw my son with a hammer, not a play hammer, but a real one. "Stop!" I yelled on impulse.

Calmly he turned and looked at me. "What are you doing?" I asked in disbelief.

Gotta Love 'Em!

"I'm just fixing the washing machine," he explained without a care in the world.

"No, it is not broken, and you are not the guy to fix it!" I said in desperation. "We don't ever use a hammer on our washing machine." I wanted to cry, I wanted to yell. I thought about "airing my dirty laundry." Instead, I took a breath and asked him if he might go find a play hammer and only use it on the soft couch.

I surveyed the damage as he left the room in search of his plastic toolbox and tools. Our washer looked as though it had been in a hail storm. As my fingers grazed the dents, I felt the anger building inside. These could never be fixed. I noticed the chipped paint and realized this washer would forever carry those marks as reminders. And then, thankfully, a fresh voice of reason took over. Just as these marks are forever and will leave a lasting mark, so too will your words and reaction. Whoa! Now that was a sobering thought. What would I remember each time I saw those dents—the way I lost my temper and blew it? Or the day I kept control and showed love? What lasting "mark" would I leave for my little boy to remember? Would he have the picture of his mother in an angry fit, or would he learn about self-control? I took a deep breath and started counting silently. Let's see, count my blessings .... Yes, I was glad that it had been the washer and not a sibling!

Next time you get frustrated and feel tempted to "air your dirty laundry," take a deep breath. Count to 10—or to 25, if you are really upset. Then try to think of things you can be grateful for. The little eyes that watch us each day can take in far more than we might imagine. They learn from our example.

LOAD LIGHTENER

November 20 is Air Your Dirty Laundry Day. I wouldn't encourage you to cut loose on this day, but how about some awareness? Maybe this would be a good opportunity to catch the "dirty laundry" you might air in your home. It is easy for a spirit of negativity and discouragement to start. Nothing smells better than fresh laundry and a joyful spirit.

Jami Kirkbride lives on a Wyoming ranch. Her inspiration comes from everyday adventures with her husband Jeff and their four children.

Gotta Love 'Em!

PRINTS CHARMING

Sherry G. Thomas

Blessed with three beautiful baby boys over the previous six years, there was no denying that time was a precious commodity in our household. But I could put off one task no longer: Something *had* to be done about my laundry room.

Since moving into our home when our first-born was only four months old, there had been as much painting, decorating, and furnishing as our shoestring budget would allow. Now, I was finally down to my last room—my least favorite of them all. But, how to go about decorating a space that really wasn't a room at all, but merely a pass-through from our backyard into the kitchen area? One that was constantly overflowing with muddy shoes, jackets, and toys that barely made it inside the back door before being tossed aside, and in which I simply hated spending time doing the laundry? Those were the questions running through my head for weeks on end.

The idea came out of nowhere: Not only would I resign myself to the fact that our laundry room was the closest thing to a real mud room we would ever have, I would embrace that realization by putting muddy handprints and footprints all over the wall! I wish I had been holding the camera the moment I revealed those plans to my husband. We could have made a killing on a credit card commercial with the "priceless" look on his face.

Armed with a bucket of "mud" paint, I lined up my subjects. My husband helped each of our boys, one by one, apply their muddy handprints as a border near the ceiling. He and I applied our own sets of prints right alongside theirs. Then it was time for a row of footprints along the wall near the floor and, finally, the finishing touch: a row of

141

hooks mounted on "mud"—painted boards running the length of the entire wall—the perfect solution for the outerwear that had once littered the floor and tops of the washer and dryer.

What a great day it turned out to be as we took turns dipping our hands and feet in the "mud," then stepping back to admire our handiwork. Little did I realize the other types of imprints that would linger long after that day ended.

On each dreaded laundry day, staring at the boys' prints for long minutes at a stretch, I would begin to catch myself smiling in spite of the chore ahead. I started spending more time folding their clothes as I paused to study each finger and toe individually; reflecting on how much growth was taking place right before my eyes—and appreciating the daily reminder. And I beamed whenever a group would gather at our house; inevitably, someone would ask to escort a new visitor in the crowd to my laundry room to see the unique borders.

Only now, more than 15 years after the day we "muddied" up our hands and feet to decorate the laundry room wall, do I understand the full implications of our project. I've come to realize that the purpose of those little hands and feet was always to leave prints—not just on my wall, but also on all the hearts they touch. And that's what happened—and is happening still—on my heart and their daddy's heart, and even on all those who have admired my laundry room wall through the years.

Yes, the rooms in my home have been decorated and redecorated many times through the years. But the heart prints my children are leaving behind will remain forever. With that thought in mind, laundry does not seem quite so mundane.

Gotta Love 'Em!

LOAD LIGHTENER

Why not invent a laundry area of your own that will serve as a reminder to appreciate each day you are given with your children? Incorporate their handprints as a design on the cabinetry or walls of your own room. Or transfer the age-old tradition of hanging their artwork on your refrigerator to the washer and dryer, rotating new pieces often. How about painting the bottom half of one wall with blackboard paint and allowing them to leave notes and drawings for you whenever the mood strikes? Who knows? You may just end up looking at the chore in a whole new way.

Sherry G. Thomas has no passion for laundry—but for writing, she does. She was published recently in P31 Woman *magazine. She lives in Midland, Texas.*

PRAYER PUPPY

Michelle Diercks

You could hear the sweet little voice reciting the common bedtime prayer, "Now I lay me down to sleep, I pray the Lord my soul to keep, the angels watch me through the night, until I wake from morning light."

The words were coming from "Prayer Puppy," the constant companion of our son Jacob when he was a year old. The tiny, light blue and white stuffed dog that prayed sported many "smudges of love"—that's what I called the stains of tears and milk, particles of food, and, at times, the clear or not-so-clear markings of a runny nose. At first, those smudges on the animal's fur disappeared with the swipe of a damp sponge or washcloth. But the smudges eventually got so thick that sponge baths weren't helping any longer. My husband and I knew it would soon be time for Prayer Puppy to take a full-blown bath. Afraid of what would happen to that puppy's precious little voice if its voicebox was immersed, we put it off the big bath day as long as we could.

One night as I was drifting into the last few minutes of wakefulness, I heard a loud howl. I dashed across the hall to Jacob's room to find my son sick with the stomach flu; the evidence of his illness covered poor Prayer Puppy from his floppy ears to his adorable little feet. Jacob didn't want to let go of his bedtime buddy—whose colors were now unrecognizable—but we knew the time had come for Prayer Puppy to the meet the washing machine. When I lifted him out of the washer, I was pleased to see that he was clean and smelled fresh once again. As I hung him gently to dry overnight, I wondered if his voice would ever be the same.

The next morning, you could see the delight on Jacob's

144

face as he hugged his squeaky-clean pal and immediately pressed the puppy's paw to listen to the sweet prayer. We heard a raspy voice instead of an angelic one. Poor Prayer Puppy had become "Wheezy Puppy"! He was in desperate need of an oxygen tank.

Jacob, however, was oblivious to the wretched noises; he was thrilled to simply have his prayer partner back. Eventually, Prayer Puppy lost his voice altogether, but the sweet bedtime prayer still resounds within the walls of our home in the cherubic voice of Jacob.

Jacob found comfort in listening to the voice of his beloved friend as he would fall asleep at night. That makes me wonder: *Does Jacob find comfort in my voice? Is my voice always pleasant and are my words loaded with love? Or do I magnify the pressures and burdens of life through my words and actions?*

"Do not let any unwholesome talk come out of your mouths, but only what is helpful for building others up according to their needs, that it may benefit those who listen" (Ephesians 4:29).

SUDSY SUGGESTION

As you're folding the following clothes for your children, offer these prayers:

Shirts – May their hearts always be filled with love for God and others.

Pants – May their bodies grow healthy and strong.

Socks – May the Lord walk with them and guide their paths.

Undergarments – May they maintain purity in body and mind.

Michelle Diercks lives in eastern Iowa with her husband and two little boys. She keeps busy by homeschooling and is training to become a medical transcriptionist.

DREAM MACHINES

Judy Dippel

"When I approach a child he inspires in me two sentiments: Tenderness for what he is, and respect for what he may become." —Louis Pasteur

I threw the last pile of clothes into my washer. My granddaughters were visiting this weekend, so they were small clothes—dresses and T-shirts, shorts and socks in every shade of the rainbow. Closing the door of my front-loading washer, I had a new revelation: Washers and dryers are dream machines.

An odd thought, perhaps, but I think you'll agree. Within these machines lies much more to treasure than the workings of ordinary household appliances. Churning and spinning within washers and dryers is tangible evidence of real life with children and life with grandchildren. Clothes can be the evidence of earthly dreams, denoting who children are or who they hope to become.

My machines have been filled with children's garb for over thirty years. During that time, I've discovered that their laundry personifies them. It vividly portrays heartfelt gifts and passions—my dreams for them and their dreams for themselves.

I pushed the "start" button and the predictable rhythmic splashing of my washer began. At the same time, immense love for my young granddaughters flowed over me. An exciting new cycle of life had begun with them.

A grin spread across my face as I watched five-year-old Olivia's blue princess dress slide across the window as the water soaked into it. Just this morning, she had paraded in front of the mirror wearing this satiny dress.

Gotta Love 'Em!

Eyes sparkling, she had admired herself, obviously very satisfied. The plastic silver crown, dangling earrings, elbow-length gloves and wobbly plastic heels were all the confirmation she needed: she was a princess!

I glanced from the colored, water-soaked clothes in the washer to the dry white clothes I'd piled on the laundry table. I was enjoying pausing in my sentimental feelings, but I'd best get on with it! I needed to get the whites folded since they incessantly reproduce.

Today, this chore wasn't a burden because I used the time to let my mind linger on thoughts of the children I love. As I did so, my heart generated unexpected memories and my imagination reminisced about clothes washed from days long past: baby blankets, toddler's bib overalls, Disney pajamas, and a special red, tattered Superman cape. The team uniforms in various sizes—bright-colored tee-ball shirts, baggy basketball shorts, sweaty track socks, and chlorine-faded swimsuits. I thought too of my daughter's colorful flag team costumes, and my son's treasured camouflage pants and jackets that he still wears, only in bigger sizes.

Suddenly, my granddaughters' sweet, constant chattering came from down the hall, jolting me back to the present. "I'm in here!" I shouted. At five and three years old, the sound of the girls' enthusiastic voices is music to my ears.

The pair came bopping through the door. "We found you, Grandma!" Olivia and Ella simultaneously chirped.

"Hey girls, what's up?" I smiled down at them, briefly thinking of the good things I hoped were yet to come in their lives.

I watched as the front-loading washer drew their attention away from me. Fascinated, they stared at their clothes swirling. Their excitement grew as they watched their favorite clothes swish gently to and fro in the splashing water. Their little-girl smiles reflected right back at them from the glass doors.

I paused to watch the "magic" they saw, and asked, "Did you know these are dream machines? Let's dream about what you want to do next time you wear the clothes we see!"

"Grandma, look!" Olivia called out as my big striped T-shirt suddenly floated across the dryer window. "I slept in that last night. I want to again tonight!"

"OK," I smiled.

More animated Olivia spoke up again: "Ella, look! My blue princess dress! Let's build a castle."

"Ooh . . . my leopard pajamas." Olivia's mouth puckered the words. Seconds later, "There they are again! I'm going to draw a jungle next time I wear them."

Scrunching up the last pair of white socks, I called out, "Lunchtime!" The girls turned and darted to the kitchen. I switched out the light, but contentedly thought, *today is only the beginning of their dreams.*

LAUNDRY'S LIFE LESSON

Take pleasure in your children's dreams and their laundry. It is "show and tell" of the people they are today and who they may become tomorrow. Life, love, and laundry will keep on, so delight in each of them. And as you do so, let your heartfelt dreams for your children spin on!

Judy Dippel is a Celebrate Moms' Team Member and lives in Oregon.

DON'T REPEAT EVERYTHING YOU HEAR

Kathy Firkins

Continually waving away the smoke billows from my grandmother's cigarette, I talked non-stop. I loved spending time with Grandma Grace. This particular morning she was staying with my sister and me while my mom was out shopping and dad was at work.

We sat at the small kitchen table trying to finish breakfast, and as she listened intently to my chatter, she slowly sipped her coffee and looked into my eyes, her cigarette smoke circling through the air above our heads.

Because I was only six years old, I can't remember the details of that conversation that day, but I do remember when Grandma Grace got up to rinse her coffee cup, I jumped up to follow her. I loved tagging behind her everywhere she went because I was afraid I might miss an opportunity to talk to her or instruct her on how "Mommy does this" or "Dad does that."

She quietly walked into the laundry room and started to pull the warm, cozy sheets from the dyer and set them in the basket close to my feet. I could feel the heat wafting up towards my face as I gazed up at her while she worked. She was thin and well dressed, and she always wore an apron tied snugly around her petite hips. Her olive complexion and fair hair were always well groomed. I thought she was simply beautiful. When she bent over to place the damp towels into the dryer, her face came near mine. I glanced into her eyes and then noticed her most unattractive feature—the cigarette dangling from her two pursed lips.

"Grandma Grace?" I questioned.

"What, child?"

"Why do you smoke?" Not waiting on an answer, I

pressed on. "You know, my daddy says smoking is a disgusting habit and he wished you wouldn't smoke in his house."

I don't recall her specific response, but I do remember that she simply finished up the laundry chore and carried on with the routines of the rest of our day. Looking back, I realize my comment might have been hurtful, yet she didn't scold me; she realized that I had been repeating something I had heard from someone else.

Not long after this visit, my whole family, including Grandma Grace, piled in the car to make the long journey across Texas to visit my uncle for Thanksgiving. Several hours before our first rest stop, my Grandmother remarked, "I better not light up; it might offend someone."

My parents, looking puzzled, asked her what she meant. When she answered that I had mentioned smoking was a disgusting habit, and that my father would rather her not smoke, they looked at me as they realized what must have happened. I had talked "out of turn."

I knew instantly that I would be in trouble, and soon enough the lectures began. They used many words to try and rein in my wayward tongue, but the refrain was always the same: "Don't repeat everything you hear, and don't share everything you know."

Sadly, Grandma Grace's most unattractive feature—the cigarette dangling from her lips—ultimately cut her life short and robbed my siblings and me of the chance to get to know her even better. However, the lesson I learned after my gossip in the laundry room has stuck with me ever since: "Don't repeat everything you hear, and don't share everything you know."

Gotta Love 'Em!

LAUNDRY'S LIFE LESSONS

"Gossip is a sort of smoke that comes from the dirty tobacco-pipes of those who diffuse it: it proves nothing but the bad taste of the smoker." —George Eliot

TIPS FOR HOLDING YOUR TONGUE

Consider what you might say if that person were standing right there.

Act as a "stop gossip agent." Speak up when others gossip. Say, "I don't feel comfortable talking about Kathy this way." Walk away or change the subject.

Need more gossip stop help? Check out Dr. Michael D. Stedler's book, *Stop the Runaway Conversation.*

Kathy Firkins is a Celebrate Moms' Team Member and lives in Texas.

LAUNDERING WITH LOVE

Jami Kirkbride

Giggles trailed from the boys' room. They warmed my heart. This, in my opinion, is the best part of mothering—watching, or in this case listening, to the children interact. They have such a variety of ways they relate. And no, it isn't always perfect.

Earlier, they had been downstairs playing and things hadn't been going well. A game of football turned into something more like keep-away. Finally, frustration sent our youngest son, Jackson, into a meltdown.

"I just want a turn, and you won't let me," he had said between sobs. At three years of age, this broke his heart.

I heard the older boys trying to console the youngest, maybe in part so that he wouldn't involve Mom.

"Sorry, sorry," our middle son, Carter, pleaded. "I really am sorry. Can I do something for you, huh? Can I do a job for you?"

I tried to contain my laughter when I recognized my discipline technique—assigning chores to transgressors—in their interaction. Deciding it was time to intervene, I came around the corner and asked the boys what happened. Taylor, our oldest, filled me in.

"Yes," he admitted, "I knew he was getting frustrated, and I didn't do anything to help him out."

"Well, Carter and Taylor, I think you know what will happen then. You will both earn a respect job," I informed them. They knew what that meant. In our home, when someone disrespects another person, we give them an assigned job—a job that would really belong to the one they disrespected. This allows them the chance to practice respect and care. "Carter, you will sort all of Jackson's laundry. Taylor, you will wash it. Then you can both put his things away."

Later, as I overheard the boys putting the laundry away, I could hear signs that the injured relationship was being mended. "Here, Buddy, can you put this one over there?" the 10-year-old asked the 4-year-old. I loved hearing them call each other pet names.

And, as the last of the clothes was being put away, "Thanks for doing my laundry," young Jackson said with gratitude as he watched his older brothers work. He had already forgotten about their offense and was feeling blessed in return for their care.

The boys came bouncing out of the room and asked for another chance to play football. "Please, Mom," Taylor said with a smile. "We'll make sure that everyone gets a turn."

"Yeah," the other two chimed in.

"Okay, go ahead," I agreed. Somehow I believed them. At least I knew they wouldn't want to do another load of laundry too soon.

SUDSY SUGGESTION

Respect jobs can be given when one member of the family disrespects another. The person who has shown disrespect is given the opportunity to practice showing respect by doing a task that would normally be the other person's responsibility—empty the trash, make beds, wash sinks, or do laundry. This may prove to be an effective way to get the children to work together and learn to show each other respect more often.

Follow these tips to set up a "respect job" system:
1. Notice when disrespect is shown in your home.
2. Figure out what jobs you will use.

3. Explain the system to the kids.
4. Use consistency as you assign respect jobs.
5. Remember, a respect job received in anger is disrespect!

Jami Kirkbride lives on a Wyoming ranch. Her inspiration comes from everyday adventures with her husband Jeff and their four children.

SUPERHEROES TO THE RESCUE

Anna Marie Warren

Not a towel left unclean,
Not a speck of dirt in sight,
Not a sock to be found,
Not a red mixed with white.

My mom was a stay-at-home mom who did a great job of filling my brother's time and mine so that we didn't get in too much trouble. One good example was how she planned laundry day. She was very tricky, but her strategy worked: Superheroes to the rescue!

Lots of good deeds needed to be accomplished on laundry day in our little Gotham town, the Bailey house. No job was too big or too small for the dynamic duo, which was always ready for action. POW!

Our day of fighting grime in the dirty city always started with costumes that put us in the spirit of the chore. Mother would make capes from whatever clean towels we had left in the cabinet, tying or clothes-pinning them around our necks (sometimes a little too tight!). SHAZAAM! In a flash, we were instant superheroes.

Mom always made up a theme song, and we would run around the house, capes flying behind us, while she sang it loudly. When we got tired of running around, we were ready for our superhero duties. Taking laundry baskets in hand, we knew our good deed for the day was to gather all the dirty laundry (the "culprits") from each room. This became tricky when some of the offenders hid. We had to plan our attack and always be watching for those lurking in the corners and under the beds. KER POW!

As we captured the runaway socks, we placed them be-

155

hind bars—laundry baskets, of course. Some scoundrels were dirtier than others, so they needed constant surveillance. We would take turns making sure no one escaped until backup help—a.k.a. Mom—arrived. Some days, we would get to take the perpetrators all the way to the cleaning place (washing machine) and add the soap. As Mom finished each load, the superhero she judged to have the greatest strength and special powers would then carry the next basket of "culprits" into the laundry room.

While the washer and dryer did their thing, helping to rid the city of all the scum and grime, my brother and I would then go from room to room—capes flying behind us all the way—making sure that no other "crooks" were hiding. We would search in closets and in every drawer, BAM! until Mom assured us we had purged all the dirty scoundrels from Gotham City. Mission accomplished, we would take off our capes, fold them up, and put them away, at least until next week, when it would be time to—ZOWIE! —put them on again to scare out the new gang of "villains" that had ridden into town.

LAUNDRY'S LIFE LESSONS

When all the "bad elements" in our city were cleaned up for the day, we would help fold each basket of clothes, quite creatively I must admit. Thinking back, I know my mom exhibited great restraint and patience at this time because she never refolded a thing, teaching me that perfection is overrated. WHAM!

At the end of a long day of fighting grime, we would eat a strength-building lunch. Sometimes Mom would try to sneak spinach into our diets by saying it would make us strong like Popeye, and we would always have to say, "Wrong super-

Gotta Love 'Em!

hero, Mom!" Then we were down for a power nap. ZONK! These naps always helped us keep our strength up for the next time of bringing good clean fun to our dirty little laundry town.

LOAD LIGHTENER

Every day, we are called on to make decisions and choices. Our attitudes and actions reflect on those around us and help determine the outcome. Be resourceful and creative with the tasks you have been given. A positive attitude—plus a little imagination—goes a long way.

Anna Marie Warren is a Celebrate Moms' Team Member and lives in Texas.

CREEK SHOES

Judy Dippel

A gentle breeze drifted in through the kitchen window, adding a spring-fresh fragrance to the house. Breathing a sigh of relief, I walked downstairs. After a long week, the house was clean and the laundry caught up.

Whew! I'm done for today, I thought. I was excited to continue reading the mystery novel I'd started, sip some iced tea, and enjoy some time to myself while the kids played outside with friends.

Opening my book, I strolled into our family room and let out a sudden gasp. I recoiled at the sight of the wet, muddy footprints that embossed the recently vacuumed, cream-colored carpet. My heart raced as my eyes followed the path of sloppy footprints that crossed to the laundry room. I didn't have to guess who they belonged to.

"Ryan!" I yelled. He didn't answer; I checked for his rubber boots. They were gone, so I knew he was, too. Undoubtedly, the boots were now on his feet, as they should have been in the first place. Being in the creek right behind our house was his favorite activity. He'd slipped quietly inside and then quickly gone back outside, leaving an unsightly trail to follow. I was frustrated. The words that ran non-stop from me to him echoed in my head, "If you go to the creek, change into your old shoes; they're great creek shoes. If not, put on your boots!"

His grubby path ended on my recently mopped laundry room floor. I cringed again! There lay his brand new Nikes, barely recognizable with their synthetic silver and black overlay design caked in thick, brown mud from heel to toe. Blades of grass and a multitude of little rocks gave the shoes a grotesque look. A collection of creek substances had begun to cement to the bottom of the waffled sole—their promise of great traction for running and basketball disappeared in the muck. I could only hope the shoes' guarantee to "hold up even in the most rugged play" was true. To hold up in the wash is what I needed. They had also been advertised as "light" and "flexible." Hmmm . . . maybe, but they sure weren't light or flexible right now. Brown creek water oozed from them, leaving irregular puddles that looked like coffee spills around each shoe. Obviously the shoes' strategically-placed vents for breathability had a far greater use than the designers could ever have imagined: They were "flow-vents" to allow water to escape!

Sarcasm and frustration seeped into my every thought. I was angry. This meant work for me, and it meant my son wasn't being responsible or listening to a word I said.

I put aside my book and my plan to relax and read, and determined what consequences were in store for Ryan. However, even while I was conjuring up a strategy for correcting his careless actions, I was fully aware of the magnitude of his love and passion for the outdoors and every creature that lived in it—meaning this wasn't the first time, and it certainly wouldn't be the last for similar incidents throughout his childhood. Messes galore, including those made by walking, crawling, and swimming creatures of every shape and size, would be a regular occurrence in our family's laundry room at one time or another.

Years later, I admit that I remember with fondness, not frustration, my son's filthy "creek shoes"—even when they happened to be his new ones. The mud-covered sneakers tell the colorful tale of the boy who wore them and of the boy I love. Though he is often impulsive, I wouldn't want him any other way.

Laundry Tales To Lighten Your Load

LOAD LIGHTENER

Don't stress over the mess, just have lots of creek shoes available. There are incredible things to be learned with our children through nature and our environment.

For starters, check out *Ranger Rick Magazine* at www.nwf.org/kidzone.

SUDSY SUGGESTIONS

Moms, don't stress! You can clean those muddy "creek shoes" (again), or better yet, let your child do it. Simply remove the laces and throw those in with a load of laundry and hang to dry. As soon as possible, rinse the mud off the shoes with warm water. Then use a cloth, a soft toothbrush, dishwashing soap, and water to hopefully wipe them clean.

For tougher stains and for the soles, try Soft Scrub. With an old toothbrush, scrub the inside of the shoe in the same way. The odor and germs of the creek, pond, or mud will vanish. After you've cleaned the shoes, dry them off inside and out. To help maintain their shape and help drying, stuff the shoes with paper towels then place near—not on—a heat source. Once dry, lace up and sprinkle inside with baking powder. They'll stay fresh if your son or daughter stays out of the creek.

Judy Dippel is a Celebrate Moms' Team Member and lives in Oregon.

Endnotes

Section 2 – Unusual Discoveries

Picking Pockets by Marilyn Rockett

[1]Louise Bachelder, editor, *Little Things* (Mount Vernon, NY: The Peter Pauper Press, 1969), 22.

[2]Luke 16:10 (*Holman Christian Standard Bible*).

Section 3 – Out of Sight, Out of Mind

Dressing for Service by Angie Peters

Article adapted from *Stay-at-Home Mom's Devotions To Go* by Angie Peters.

Section 4 – Hanging Out, Hanging Up, and Hanging On

Never Throw in the Towel by Bonnie Wheat

From *Why Do We Say It?: The Stories Behind the Words, Expressions and Clichés We Use,* Castle Books, 1985

The Celebrate Moms' Team

Celebrate Moms, Inc. started in 2005 as an online conference and retreat center for moms. When founders Melissa Howell and Angie Peters realized that the ministry vision extended beyond their abilities, they quickly recruited the talents of several other women to form the Celebrate Moms' Team.

The team is comprised of women from across the United States who are currently speaking and writing in their respective areas; representing a kaleidoscope of church denominations and mothering stages. Their combined experience, unique personalities and sincere dedication enable the team to meet the needs of mothers everywhere. You can reach all of the team members and guest contributors through the Celebrate Moms ministry website.

Judy Dippel is a writer and speaker with a passion to share with women how they can strive towards living out God's best in their lives. Married since 1970, she is a mother, grandmother, and lifelong Oregonian. Her expanse of career experience includes work in the fields of medicine, education, international adoption, and corporate America. Judy feels being a mother is by far the most challenging job she's ever had—it inspired her first book, *Refreshing Hope in God: A Mother's Journey of Joy and Pain*. She's contributed stories to several compilation books and has other book proposals in process.

Kathy Firkins inspires, equips and trains women (and those who live, work or worship with them) to be the confident, efficient and purposeful women God created them to be! She is a productivity specialist, speaker and writer. Kathy speaks on all subjects related to organization or productivity as well as teen pregnancy, abstinence, and God's grace. She also motivates companies with over 20 corporate training modules. Kathy calls Midland, TX home where she lives on a small farm with husband Justin and their three angelic children.

Jill Hart is the founder of an online community called Christian Work at Home Moms. The site is dedicated to providing work-at-home moms with opportunities to promote their businesses while at the same time providing them spiritual encouragement and articles. Jill and her husband Allen of Christian Work at Home Dads reside in Nebraska with their two children. Jill also hosts an Internet radio show, Christian Work at Home Moment.

Melinda Hines has been married to Cory, a pastor, for 10 years and they have two children, Mackenzie and Caleb. She has written for *MomSense, Focus on Your Child, InTouch, LifeLine Journal, Radiantmag.com, Simplejoy.org,* and *CBN.com.* She is a features writer for the *Waxahachie Daily Light, Waxahachie Magazine* and *Now Magazine.* Melinda is a staff writer and podcast author for *www.inspiredmoms.com.* She is a CLASS graduate, former teacher and the founder and coordinator of Moms On Mission. She enjoys speaking to moms' groups and at women's retreats. Melinda's book, *Operation Mom – Winning the Mommy Wars,* will be out in September 2007.

Tonya Holter is a wife, mother, pediatric registered nurse, Bible teacher, and speaker. She is married to her high school sweetheart, Troy, and they have three beautiful children, Tyler, 17, Lauren, 14, and Kyle, 10. Troy is a full time student pastor and they make their home in Sheridan,

Arkansas. Tonya's passion has always been women's ministry; focusing on young women and moms. Her greatest desire is to show women the extreme blessings that come from extreme obedience to the Lord.

Melissa Howell is a blended family mother of seven children. As the co-founder and Executive Director of Celebrate Moms, she spends most days encouraging, equipping and inspiring other moms. Melissa was privileged to serve on the faculty of the 2006 Glorieta Christian Writers' Conference. In addition to writing the bi-weekly Celebrate Moms newsletter, her work has been featured in *The Mobile Press Register, Bay News, The WC Magazine, PeopleofFaith.com*, and *InspiredMoms.com*. Melissa and her husband, Gary, were married at midnight on New Year's Eve of 2000. They live in Grand Bay, AL with their children.

Sandy McKeown is a mother of five, grandmother of two and "Mentor of Many" (M.O.M.). She is a contributing author to *One Year Life Verse Devotional* and *Chicken Soup for the Chocolate Lover's Soul* and speaks approximately twice a month for various groups both alone and with the Celebrate Moms' team. These include: autism and ADHD seminars, women's groups, men's groups, church groups, and college classrooms. Sandy and her husband teach pre-marriage and marriage sessions, and mentor other parents who are discovering the challenges of raising children while struggling to keep their marriages strong. Sandy lives in Iowa with her husband and their two youngest children.

Angie Peters, co-founder of Celebrate Moms, thought she was closing the door on her writing career forever 17 years ago when she quit her job as a journalist to become a stay-at-home mom. It turns out that God had other plans. He used her experiences during that transition from work to home to inspire her first book, *Celebrate Home: Encouragement & Tips for Stay-at-Home Parents.* Since then, she's written several other books, including in-depth study guides on the lives of David and Solomon, to be released next year. Angie celebrates life with her husband and their three children at their hectic but happy home in central Arkansas.

Sandra Stanford has been a Christian for almost 25 years. She and her wonderful husband, David, have been married since 1988 and reside in Titusville, FL. They have two precious children, Anna Beth, and Jonathan. Sandra has been active in her church, a multi-cultural, interdenominational fellowship, having led a Women's Bible Study for several years. Currently, she is a Bible teacher, a speaker on a radio program, participates on a Nursing Home ministry team, is a mentor in the MOPS ministry, and has ministered to single moms. Next to Jesus and her family, ministering to women is Sandra's greatest desire.

Anna Marie Warren desires to lead others to see themselves as God sees them, no matter where they have been or what they have done. She has an active ministry as a speaker, worship leader, writer, and personality trainer. She speaks and leads worship at conferences, retreats, and churches nationwide and has been privileged to travel around the world to share God's love. She writes monthly articles and has contributed to several compilation books due out in 2007. She is married to Scott and is mother to four beautiful daughters.

Karen H. Whiting has a heart for encouraging women to creatively connect to God, treasure family life, and bring the presence of Christ into the home. As a mother of five, she learned to delegate laundry duties early on and seldom does it herself. Karen has authored ten books, hundreds of articles, and is a contributing writer for *Focus on Your Child*. Her work has appeared in numerous publications, including *Focus on the Family, Today's Christian Woman*, and *Christian Parenting Today*. Karen hosted Puppets on Parade, an educational television series and will have four new books released soon.

Cassandra Woods is an inspirational writer who has seen God's Word become real in her own life. She finds great joy in sharing God's love with other women and encouraging them to develop an intimate relationship with God. She resides in Alabama with her awesome husband and four children.